Uncle Sam: The Man and the Legend

Uncle

THE MAN AND

Sam:
THE LEGEND

By ALTON KETCHUM

HILL AND WANG * NEW YORK

Design and typography by Myrtle Powell
Set in Linotype Times Roman
Manufactured in the United States of America:
Composition by Lettick Typografic, Inc.
Printed by Colorgraphic Offset Company
Bound by American Book-Stratford Press

To HERBERT RICHARDS NOXON
whose Uncle Sam pleased the old gentleman himself

Foreword

It is a paradox that Uncle Sam had been around for 137 years before the U. S. Government decided to do anything about him. As often happens with characters who grow right out of the grass roots, Uncle Sam took over without any official sanction, rules and regulations for display, or acts of Congress prohibiting misuse of, etc. Despite keen competition from a number of other candidates, he managed to survive through war and peace, hard times and lean. There was something about him that was timeless and perennially satisfying.

My own interest in him began one day in July, 1950, with a call from the International Press and Publications Division of the Department of State. The voice said that the State Department was looking for a definitive Uncle Sam. It seemed that people frequently came in to American embassies and consulates overseas wanting to know how Uncle Sam should really look. Not the foreign caricatures, many of which made him into all sorts of fool and ogre. They wanted to know how *Americans* saw him. A specific request had come from Johannesburg, South Africa. The State Department man had inspected all the Uncle Sams he could find in the Library of Congress. But none of them really measured up to the Department's idea of what Uncle Sam ought to look like: benign, friendly, yet firm — a character one would like to meet and know. At this po'nt they had run across a booklet called *The Miracle of America*, which I had written for a campaign of the Advertising Council. It was a popular description of the American economic system; in it a family had come to Uncle Sam for information and advice. The Uncle Sam pictured in it was exactly the one the Department wanted. Who was the artist, and did I think he would be willing to do a full-length version? I said his name was Herbert Noxon, he was probably the best-known poster designer in the country, he was then on vacation somewhere up in Connecticut, and yes, I was pretty sure he would be glad to oblige.

He was and he did. A special-delivery letter reached Mr. Noxon, and in due course there arrived back in my office four rough sketches of Uncle Sam on hotel note paper, done in various attitudes to indicate degrees of the benign, the friendly, and the firm. The one we liked best was, luckily, the one Washington did, too. It was finished up, and Mr. Noxon received the thanks of a grateful Government, which he framed, with the original, and hung in his office at McCann-Erickson. And that is how the Uncle Sam who represents us to the world came to be.

All this made me wonder what other versions of Uncle Sam had appeared through the years, how he began in the first place, and where he had gotten his name and fame. I found, to my surprise, that there had been a *real* Sam Wilson — that he had lived in Troy, N. Y. during the War of 1812, and that it had been through constant reference to him that the whole Uncle Sam concept had started. I went to Troy, as well as Mason, N. H., where Sam Wilson had lived his early years, and to Arlington, Massachusetts, his birthplace. I pored over local facts and legends about him, and visited the principal sites of his career. Research in Troy, Arlington, New York City and Washington filled in many missing parts of the story. In the process I dug up stacks of old cartoons and emblematic lore bearing on the early representations of America, both before and after Uncle Sam. The pile got higher and higher, till after a few years there was enough for a book. And here it is.

ALTON KETCHUM

viii

Acknowledgments

Acknowledgments are due the following, who have helped in ways great and small to follow the facts about Uncle Sam to their beginnings: to Miss Elizabeth Orton Jones, of Mason, N. H., whose wide knowledge of local history and Uncle Sam lore has proved both helpful and stimulating; to Mr. Archie Eaton of Greenville, N. H.; to Mr. Clarence Jackson of Denver, Colo., Mrs. Louise McLeod of Detroit, Mich., and Mr. C. W. Sheldon of Ozark, Ark., all descendants of Samuel Wilson, and to Mr. R. M. Brockett of Kansas City, Mo., who married Samuel Wilson's great-granddaughter Helen Marion Sheldon, for their aid in tracing relationships.

Special thanks go to Mr. Art Wood, editorial cartoonist of the *Pittsburgh Press*, for lending so many fine examples from his Uncle Sam cartoon collection; also to Dean Burton W. Marvin of the William Allen White School of Journalism, University of Kansas at Lawrence, Kan., and Miss Jean McKnight, Archivist-Librarian there, for a number of Uncle Sams by noted cartoonists of today and yesterday.

Valuable contributions were made by Mr. Frederick R. Goff, chief of the rare book division, Library of Congress, who provided the first known reference to Uncle Sam, and by Miss Virginia Daiker, Reference Librarian at the Library of Congress. Records of Samuel and Ebenezer Wilson's contract with Elbert Anderson were sought out and photostated by Mr. Victor Gondos, Jr., Archivist in charge of the Old Army Branch, National Archives and Records Service, Washington, D. C. The interested cooperation of Miss Fanny C. Howe, Librarian of the Troy (N. Y.) Public Library, supplied much of the basic data of the Uncle Sam story, including the important file assembled by Miss Jessie F. Wheeler while reference librarian there. Constant sources of good advice have been the librarians in the American History, Print, and Art sections of the New York Public Library; also those in the Reference and Print rooms of the New York Historical Society.

The large resources of the New York Genealogical and Biographical Society have been generously offered and used. Mrs. Dorothy L. Hart of the Robbins Library, Arlington, Mass., helped greatly by locating early references to the Wilson family, and old maps of Arlington. Mr. James J. Golden, Town Clerk of Arlington, verified Samuel Wilson's birth date. Mr. Clarence S. Brigham, Director of the American Antiquarian Society, Worcester, Mass., supplied a print of "Uncle Sam in Danger," the first cartoon to show the character. Mr. William F. Wilson of Albany, N. Y., suggested numerous sources in that area. Mr. Warren Howard Russell of Arlington, Mass., a lineal descendant of the Russell family who bought Edward Wilson's property there, furnished helpful information. Valuable aid was given by Mr. Dwight Marvin, former editor of the *Troy Record*, Mr. Alton T. Sliter, present editor, and Mr. J. Arthur Viger, advertising director. Mr. John J. Demers, Troy military artist and historian, graciously permitted use of his drawings. The Rev. L. V. W. Hutton, Pastor of the First Baptist Church of Catskill, N. Y., helped to fill in facts about Samuel Wilson's sojourn there. Mrs. Gordon Gorham of Mt. Kisco, N. Y., answered questions about her grandfather, Rev. George Franklin Merriam, who is reported to have settled Samuel

Wilson's estate. Miss Charlotte D. Conover, Librarian of the New Hampshire Historical Society, Concord, N. H., established some pertinent facts about Uncle Sam's early career, particularly the service boy story.

Miss R. Shevin of the Argosy Book Stores, New York City, turned up many rare prints illustrating the evolution of American symbolism. Mr. Samuel Stager of the Cadmus Book Shop, Mr. Samuel Loveman of the Bodley Book Shop, Mr. George Stair of Brentano's, and Mr. Murray Dauber of the Dauber & Pine book store provided much-needed sources and periodicals.

Mr. Albert Bearup, Managing Editor of the *Albany Times Union*, sent a photographer throughout that area looking for a picture of Samuel Wilson. Mr. John Fischetti, editorial cartoonist of Newspaper Enterprise Association, helped greatly in securing cooperation of other leading cartoonists. Mr. Louis C. Jones, Director of the New York State Historical Association, gave valuable advice. Extensive quotations were kindly permitted by Mr. Frank Weitenkampf, whose researches in Uncle Sam history are a *must* for anyone working on the subject. Mr. Albert B. Corey, State Historian of New York, and Mr. William G. Tyrrell of his staff verified dates and data.

Interesting background information came from Rep. Dean P. Taylor of Troy, N. Y., concerning his resolution passed by the House of Representatives on July 20, 1959, recognizing Uncle Sam's grave in Oakwood Cemetery, Troy, as a national shrine; also from Rep. Leo W. O'Brien of Albany, N. Y., who co-sponsored the resolution, and from Rep. Wayne M. Aspinall, Chairman of the House Committee on Insular and Interior Affairs, which reported the resolution favorably.

Others who helped the project along include Mrs. Theodore A. Wilson, Delmar, N. Y., Miss Helen Waterbury, Librarian of *The Albany Knickerbocker News*, Miss Janet MacFarlane of the Albany Institute of History and Art, Mr. Maxson Holloway, Director of the Rensselaer County Historical Society, Troy, N. Y., Mr. Francis P. Kimball, publicity director of the New York State Department of Commerce, Albany, N. Y., Mrs. Alden W. Smith of Doylestown, Pa., Miss Gladys Ladu and Miss Gertrude H. Kleinhans, assistant librarians of the New York State Library, Albany, N.Y., Dean Earl English of the University of Missouri School of Journalism, Columbia, Mo., Mr. Lynn H. Gamble, advertising director of the *San Francisco Chronicle*, Mr. Sam Hill, national advertising manager of the *Washington Post-Times-Herald*, Mr. James T. Abajian, of the California Historical Society Library, and Mr. Bradford M. Hill, supervisor of reference and research services, Boston Public Library.

Miss Ruth Cassell, Mr. Gus Scheuer, Mr. Keith Reynolds, and Miss Leyla Sefa of McCann-Erickson gave bountifully of their time and effort. Particular recognition is due Miss Myrtle Powell, whose skillful editing contributed so much throughout the book. Finally, the encouragement of the author's wife Robyna and his daughter Debby, and their patience in hearing of Uncle Sam's exploits for nearly a decade, should be gratefully recorded.

*   *   *

The author is indebted to the following for permission to reproduce illustrations and cartoons as noted. The numbers in parentheses following the names are *Figure* references: Albany Institute of History and Art (51); James T. Berryman (122); Herbert Block (10)); Columbus *Dispatch* (113); Controller of Her Britannic Majesty's Stationery Office, British Crown copyright (110); Curtis Brown, Ltd. (120); *Deccan Herald* (138); John J. Demers (38); Edmund Duffy (117); D. R. Fitzpatrick (114); James Montgomery Flagg (109); Langhorne Gibson (112); Grau Sala (artist) and Librairie Plon (126); *London Daily Express* (9); Edwin Marcus (121); *Miami Herald* (19); New York Herald Tribune, Inc., © 1932 (118); New York State Historical Association, Cooperstown (32); New York *World-Telegram* (2); Herbert R. Noxon (title page); Lillian P. Packer (7); Press Publishing Co. (11, 107); Punch, © (4, 64, 65, 66, 67, 68, 69, 77, 78, 79, 80, 81, 102, 132); Norman Rockwell (115); Fred O. Seibel (5, 123); Kendall Vintroux (1); Yardley — Baltimore *Sun* (140); and NEA Service, Inc. (141).

Quoted matter is reprinted with the following permissions: *Encyclopedia Britannica*, pp. 120-21; from *Low's Autobiography* by David Low, with permission of Simon and Schuster, Inc., p. 121; from *Time Exposure* by William Henry Jackson, copyright 1940 by William Henry Jackson, published by G. P. Putnam's Sons, New York, pp. 43-44; and Frank Weitenkampf, pp. 132-33.

Contents

		page
	Foreword	vii
1:	Symbols — The Shorthand of Ideas	1
2:	America Seeks Its Symbols	10
3:	Yankee Doodle Grows Up	27
4:	A Matter of Pride	34
5:	The Legend Is Born	38
6:	A Man Called Uncle Sam	45
7:	The Legend Grows	59
8:	Rumblings of Civil War	70
9:	Uncle Sam and Abe Lincoln	80
10:	The Era of Nast	87
11:	Uncle Sam's Progress	95
12:	The Jaundiced-Eye View	111
13:	Uncle Sam Today	120
	References	125
	Bibliography	135
	Index	139

Uncle Sam: The Man and the Legend

1: Symbols - The Shorthand of Ideas

To most Americans the United States without Uncle Sam would seem like Christmas without Santa Claus. He has been a part of the national scene for as long as any of us can remember, and it is hard to imagine a time when he did not exist. We are inclined to take him for granted, even though we are aware that in today's world he is more important than ever before. To the poor Kaffir in South Africa, who has only a vague idea where the United States *is,* to the jade merchant in Hong Kong, the sheepherder in Argentina — Uncle Sam is the personal, human embodiment of the U.S.A. Presidents enter and depart, but Uncle Sam goes on indefinitely.

Once when we were small and relatively isolated, it may not have been too significant what the rest of the world thought of the old fellow in the striped pants and the congress gaiters. But today he represents the nation which has attained to a position of power without parallel in history. He is the leader of the free world; millions depend on him for aid and inspiration. This is not wholly new, for America has long been the land of promise. But lately his responsibilities have become staggering. Today he is always in the limelight. And even though Uncle Sam has now had nearly 150 years of public service, the old boy seems at times to be a little overwhelmed. In this respect he simply reflects the composite reactions of us all.

His bewilderment — and ours — is dramatized in many current cartoons. Kendall Vintroux of the Charleston, West Virginia, *Gazette* (FIGURE 1) shows a rather timorous Uncle Sam, complete with moneybag. And Willard Mullin of the

1

Figure 1

New York *World-Telegram* (FIGURE 2) indicates that the job of leadership brings with it many thorny problems, not the least of which is the sharing of his substance with the less fortunate.

Uncle Sam is a symbol — a fairly recent one in the long procession of such emblems through history. Symbols are the shorthand of ideas. Man is the only symbol-using creature because he is the only animal who has learned to reason. From the earliest cave drawings to the complicated heraldic devices of the Middle Ages, signs and symbols often took the pictorial image of the object or process represented. Yet in symbolism the mystical was often found too. All the lore of astrology, that oldest of the pseudosciences, of alchemy, magic, mathematics, religion, and the world of the imagination found symbolic meanings, often obscure but none the less real. It has been pointed

out[1] that the ancient wisdom of the pagan world "went underground" early in the Christian era, to reappear in modern times in such forms as watermarks and fraternal emblems.

Man could not live without symbols. For these are the signs we set down on paper or wood — incise in rock or metal — to record the true meaning of people, ideas, and events. Language is a succession of symbols designed to convey meaning. All pictures are a step removed from reality; hence they are also part of our symbolic file. If hieroglyphics can stand for the sun, for a man, for an animal, as they did and still do for primitive peoples, then how natural to represent nations and groups as well in human, animal, or other symbolic form? And if, in simpler eras, this was an instinctive act on the part of man, in these complex times there would seem to be even more reason for it. To finite minds struggling with the multitudinous issues of modern life, the symbol is a more acceptable device than ever before. True, representing Capital as a silk-hatted plutocrat and Labor as a worker in a square paper cap may seem to be an oversimplification. Thomas Nast depicted them that way in his effective cartoon which appeared in an 1874 issue of *Harper's Weekly* (FIGURE 3). In this drawing he was trying to demonstrate their mutual interdependence.

Without such symbols to stand for groups and causes, however, abstract thought would be for many people difficult, if not impossible. The symbol is and will remain a rallying point for the like-minded, drawn to it because it expresses a viewpoint which might otherwise not be

2

expressed at all. Indeed, it may well be that we are tending more toward symbolism than away from it. This is the heyday of the engineer, whose work is represented by the symbols of mathematics. Explorers of both the atom and the universe express their ideas and conjectures in symbols almost esoteric. On every side, advertisements call upon us to remember this or that trademark or brand name. Slogans, symbolic sounds, and catchwords are dinned into our ears. A whole set of international highway direction symbols has recently been adopted for the use and convenience of motorists.

When symbols come to represent political ideas they often acquire a power that is almost frightening. They encourage the tendency to think in stereotypes. Mr. Common People, The Interests, Congress, Peace, the mailed fist — each calls up a host of well-conditioned reflexes which, when coordinated and led, make history.

Uncle Atlas

Figure 2

The symbol is often a champion, as in the case of John Bull. The example reproduced (FIGURE 4) is by Linley Sambourne, as it appeared in *Punch* in 1887. One wonders how much of the innate appeal of Winston Churchill to the British people came from his resemblance to that legendary figure. Certainly if one had been casting Squire Bull for a play, Mr. Churchill would have gotten the part. And so it is with the other national figures: the Alphonse-and-Gaston type of the comedy Frenchman, together with his female counterpart, Marianne; and Fritz, the sausage-eating German, with his meerschaum pipe and spectacles. "The bear that walks like a man" has long represented Russia. This symbol and the U. S. eagle clash in a cartoon by Fred Seibel titled "No Pushover" (FIGURE 5) which

Figure 4

Figure 3

4

appeared in the Richmond *Times-Dispatch* during the Berlin blockade of 1948. Sometimes the symbol is the conventionalized figure of a noted leader, as in the case of Gandhi for India, drawn by the Latin-American cartoonist Cardenio (FIGURE 6).

An amusing commentary on the American tendency to symbolize appeared in the New York *Mirror* during the campaign of 1956. Cartoonist Dan Packer celebrated the vote cast for Joe Smith for Vice President at the Republican convention by illustrating his welcome into the Americans Anonymous Club, of which Uncle Sam is a prominent member. (FIGURE 7).

The Apostle of Indian Freedom   Cardenio

Figure 6

Figure 5 (below)

Figure 7 (below)

Symbols may have begun as charms to ward off evil spirits. You can still see the blue hand of Fatima over the doorways of Moslem homes, put there for that purpose. It is not so different from the hex signs one sees in traveling through the beautiful Pennsylvania Dutch countryside. Often these symbols have taken the imagined shape of spirits, gods, and demons — a tendency which began in Egypt and Babylon and continued through the golden ages of Greece and Rome. Such were the Colossus of Rhodes which represented Helios, the sun god, and the twin colossi of Memnon which still sit on Egypt's Theban plain, though the temple which they guarded has long since disappeared. So also with Gog and Magog, the oft-destroyed and as often replaced giants of the Apocalypse in London's Guildhall.

In nearly every era art has joined with politics or civic ardor to create tangible evidence of the ideals upheld by philosophers and sages. Valor, virtue, industry, commerce, wisdom — evocations of these and many others stood in the temple porches or decorated the figureheads of ships. But it was not until the invention of printing that the symbol could finally come into its own. Then it could be circulated to thousands over long distances, in the form of either words, pictures, or both. At first these were mostly concerned with theology. Woodcuts told the moral tales which, as masques depicting virtues and vices, were the beginning of the modern theater. It was only a step from this to the political and social cartoon, which really came into its own in the eighteenth century, with such masters as Gillray, Rowlandson, and above all,

Hogarth. Some of the "prints," as they were then known, were incredibly gross and scurrilous. Yet, unlike newspapers, they seem to have been almost immune to prosecution. One reason may have been that these political works were so effective, as is shown by the rewards in the way of sinecures given the "etchers." The old type of "emblematical" prints, which were often keyed to legends like puzzles, were gradually transformed into caricatures, usually colored and sometimes fiendishly cruel. The illustrated joke appeared. The popularity of this new kind of expression may be judged from the fact that in London there were a number of print-sellers advertising exhibitions of caricatures — admission one shilling. Large portfolios of prints were rented out for the evening and were a necessary part of every good library. One imagines that they served the same purpose as the family photograph album and the stereopticon did in the nineties.

The first American to recognize the power of the political cartoon to sway men's minds was Benjamin Franklin. Himself a printer, he made good use of pictorial diagrams of which he is supposed to have been the author, if not the artist. One of these was "Magna Britania her Colonies Reduc'd" (FIGURE 8), which he prepared in 1774 for circulation in England. Franklin hoped that by warning the mother country of the evil effects of losing her American colonies, she might be impelled to more generous treatment of them. He predicts that if Britain is not careful, she will suffer the fate of the great Roman General Belisarius, who fell into disfavor and lived his last days

6

Figure 8

on the alms of others. Franklin shows a Britain no longer mistress of the world. She cannot use her shield and lance, for her colonial limbs have been lopped off. The British oak has been blasted, and the brooms at the mastheads of her ships signify that they are for sale. The Latin inscription on the ribbon says: "Give Belisarius a penny." Franklin often reproduced such cartoons on his letter paper. In a very real sense he was the first American propagandist.

If the symbol is natural and necessary for man, then so is the political cartoon. No better way has yet been devised of conveying in a flash, to all kinds of people, a point of view on matters of general interest. The cartoon is first cousin to the gag, that Americanized apothegm which, while it derives from the maxims of Epictetus and La Rochefoucauld, is yet a distinctive form in its own right.

Political cartoons using symbolic characters early proved to be ideal vehicles for one of the most difficult of all forms — satire. It was possible to show a whole nation in the person of one character and all Europe in a single social group. Cartoonists found that the simple idea was clearest, and achieved greatest impact. The early cartoons were as involved as a marble frieze. Later they became visual graphs, understandable instantly by anyone from nine to ninety.

The British cartoonist Strube mingled several of these symbols in 1939. Stalin,

Figure 9

Figure 11

Hitler, Mussolini, Daladier, and Chamberlain perch on their respective emblems to escape the flood, as Peace rows by in a skiff (FIGURE 9).

Ominous and memorable is the figure of Mr. Atom Bomb, introduced by Herblock of the Washington *Post* (FIGURE 10). The symbol has been used recurrently since then.

The really great cartoonists have had that rare ability to get at the true inwardness of a situation, together with a sense of timing and appropriateness which is possessed by top entertainers. And their efforts have made an impression correspondingly deep. A series of cartoons by a man like Thomas Nast could galvanize the forces of law and order to root out the Tweed Ring. Rollin Kirby, with his famous bluenose Prohibitionist (FIGURE 11), probably did as much as any single individual to bring about the repeal of the Volstead Act.

If anyone doubts the value of symbols in the modern world, let him consider the appropriation of the dove of peace by the communists during the past few years. The well-known Picasso dove displayed at communist meetings in Europe and elsewhere, has practically denied the use of that immemorial bird to the forces of freedom. Millions live and die today under the symbol of the hammer and sickle, just as other millions have for so many cen-

Figure 10

turies looked to the cross. In many minds the scar of the swastika is still raw. Yet the swastika was for untold ages a mystical sign familiar to all the peoples of the ancient world. It remained for the Nazis to pervert it into a symbol of hate and conquest.

Amid this great and growing constellation of symbols, Uncle Sam shines out as a star of the first magnitude. He *is* the United States for peoples in all parts of the world. He is our composite American personality — the symbolic projection of what our country means to us and to other nations.

2: America Seeks Its Symbols

The earliest authentic pictures of America and the people who lived there were published in 1590 by Théodore de Bry, a Flemish goldsmith and engraver. His first volume, depicting the denizens of Virginia, followed the original water colors of John White, a member of Sir Walter Raleigh's expedition of 1585. White returned in 1587 as governor of the colony. In 1591 De Bry published his engravings of pictures made by the French artist Jacques le Moyne de Morgues, who went with Laudonnière's expedition to Florida (now South Carolina) in 1564. The engravings in both these books were infinitely better than the crude woodcuts which had preceded them. They were carefully studied by cartographers engaged in making maps of the New World. They noted the frequency with which De Bry's engravings showed muscular young Indian maidens, and before long these began to find their way into the decorative cartouches which embellished the maps. Thus came into being the earliest symbol of America — the Indian girl of the Pocahontas legend. For the next century she was to be the representative of the New World, and even well into the 1700's many maps and prints continued to depict her in various attitudes as the emblem of the Americas.

Some good examples are the rotund belles on the frontispiece of Johann Ludwig Gottfried's *Historia Antipodum* (Figures 12–13), an account of the New World published at Frankfurt, Germany, in 1655. The drawings were by the well-known map engraver Matthäus Merian. Another example (Figure 14) is a title page of *America: being the latest and most accurate Description of the New*

10

Figure 12

Figure 13

World, by the noted cartographer John Ogilby, published in London in 1671. Ogilby had been a bookseller, translator, printer, dancing master, theater owner, master of the King's Revels, and lastly a geographer. A third example (FIGURE 15), printed nearly a century later (1757) by the map-making family of Robert de Vaugondy, shows that Pocahontas was still the symbol of America to the outside world in the years preceding the Revolution. It appeared in their great *Atlas Universel,* for which Mme. de Pompadour was one of the leading subscribers.

At the time of the Revolution the British colonies in America often devised their own symbols, which were displayed on the colonial banners and those of military groups. Among these the pine tree is one of the more noteworthy. The tree motif derived from the Biblical tree of life. As early as 1652, the Colony of Massachusetts had decreed that all pieces of money should bear a tree. One of these was the famous pine tree shilling. Later the American naval cruisers of the Revo-

11

AMERICA

Figure 14

12

lution were to fly at their mastheads a white flag with a green pine tree and the inscription "An Appeal to Heaven" (FIGURE 16). The Sons of Liberty met at an old elm in Hanover Square, Boston, which was known as the Liberty Tree. And it was with that in mind that Thomas Jefferson made his famous remark that the tree of liberty must be watered with the blood of patriots.

Perhaps the most popular symbol of the time was the rattlesnake, together with the slogan "Don't Tread on Me" (FIGURE 17). On one banner we find the coiled serpent added to the pine tree design. This choice was explained by one contemporary writer as follows: The rattlesnake's eye was brighter than that of any other animal, she had no eyelids and thus might be taken as a symbol of vigilance, and furthermore she never began an attack, but never surrendered when assailed. Most important, the bite of the rattlesnake was deadly. "It is curious and amazing to observe how distinct and independent of each other the rattles of this reptile are, and yet how firmly they are united together. One of these rattles, singly, is incapable of producing a sound, but the ringing of thirteen together is sufficient to alarm the boldest man living."[1]

The Navy Jack of the Revolution, flown usually from the bow, showed the rattlesnake diagonally across thirteen red and white stripes. This design was used by the South Carolina Navy. It was displayed on the *Alfred* under Commodore Esek Hopkins when he made his raid on New Providence in the Bahamas in 1776.

In connection with this extensive use of the serpent symbol by our forefathers, it

Figure 15

is significant to note some earlier uses of the sign. The Mayan and Egyptian hieroglyph for water was a zigzag or wavy line to represent the undulations of the sea. The Mayas terminated this sign in the head of a snake because of the serpentine movements of the great waters. By process of evolution this became the symbol for *spirit*. The serpent sign came to stand

13

Figure 16

Figure 17

also and almost universally for celestial wisdom, while the sloughing off of the skin signified regeneration. Moreover, the serpent was widely believed to live on even after it was cut to pieces.

The popularity and persistence of the snake device accounts for its use as early as May 9, 1754, when Franklin's famous "Join or Die" cartoon appeared in *The Pennsylvania Gazette*. The snake was divided into eight parts, each bearing the initials of one of the colonies; the slogan was intended to urge union against the French and Indians. This device was used intermittently for the next twenty years. It was revised by Isaiah Thomas for his *Massachusetts Spy* (FIGURE 18), where it appeared on July 5, 1774, this time in nine sections, with a dragon representing Great Britain. It must have struck home, for Thomas continued to run it for nine months, right under the masthead. It drew the following comment from the Tory newspaper, Rivington's New York *Gazetteer*:

Ye sons of Sedition, how comes it to pass
That America's typed by a snake — in the grass?

Figure 18 (below)

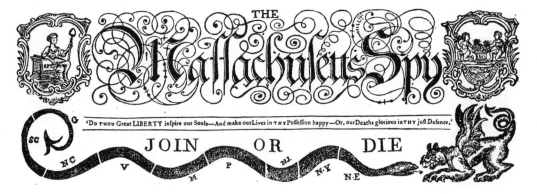

14

Figure 19

Figure 20

wisdom (FIGURE 20). In 1770 she took over from Britannia at the masthead of the Boston *Gazette*. Her shield still bore the Union Jack device, but much else of import had been added. A Phrygian liberty cap such as had been given to Roman slaves when they became freedmen now surmounts her spear. And she is opening a cage from which a bird flies toward the tree of liberty. This little tableau alone shows how outspoken the bolder spirits had become five years before the first shot was fired.

As a printer, and a publicist of no mean ability, Benjamin Franklin realized the value of such symbolic declarations. He reproduced and distributed them widely. Some of the cartoons of the period are attributed to Paul Revere. One of these (FIGURE 21) is "The Able Doctor, or America swallowing the Bitter Draught" (1775), which like many of the others was re-engraved from originals published in Britain by those sympathizing with the Revolutionists. It is interesting that America is still shown as an Indian girl, albeit with a long skirt in place of the original kirtle. A beautifully executed European engraving, "The Tea Pot Tempest," dated 1778, shows (FIGURE 22) the Pocahontas maid, with Minerva and Britannia watching a magic lantern show in which the defeat of the King's forces is predicted. Father Time presides.

In a British cartoon of 1782 (FIGURE 23), "The Reconciliation Between Britania and Her Daughter America," Pocahontas is returned to her former costume and coloration. This particular design was propaganda for the peace talks which were then proceeding.

That the symbol is still remembered in moments of national crisis is shown by the Enright cartoon "Dusting off an old heirloom" which appeared in the Miami *Herald* (FIGURE 19) in June, 1941, when war was only six months away.

The turbulent pre-Revolutionary days spawned other symbols as loyalty waned for Britannia, the Crown, and the British Lion. One which was used on both sides of the Atlantic was Minerva, goddess of

Figure 21 (above)

Figure 22 (below)

16

Figure 23

Once the Colonies had won their independence, other changes began to take place. For one thing, the dark skin lightened considerably to match the predominantly white aspect of the American population. In a French aquatint of this transition period by Berteaux, dated 1786, she is entirely white, though she still retains her Indian costume (FIGURE 24). She holds a liberty pole in one hand and a caduceus in the other. On the monument appear Louis XVI, Franklin, and "Waginston." The inscription says, "America and the Seas, O Louis! Will Remember You Their Liberator." The vanquished British lion cowers beneath her foot.

The Declaration of Independence was signed by members of the Continental Congress about two o'clock in the afternoon of July 4, 1776. Later that day Congress *"Resolved,* that Dr. Franklin, Mr. J. Adams and Mr. Jefferson be a committee to prepare a device for a Seal of the United States of America." This was the same committee, less Robert R. Livingston and Roger Sherman, which had drawn up the Declaration. The committee called upon Eugène Pierre du

17

Figure 24

Simitière, a French artist from the West Indies, to put their ideas on paper. John Adams wrote his wife on August 14:

This M. Du Simitière is a very curious man. He has begun a collection of materials for a history of this revolution. He cuts out of the newspapers every scrap of intelligence and every piece of speculation and pastes it upon clean paper, arranging them under the head of that state to which they belong, and intends to bind them up as a volume. He has

a list of every speculation and pamphlet concerning independence, and another concerning forms of government.

Adams also recorded that Du Simitière himself proposed a seal (FIGURE 25) combining

the arms of the several nations from whence America has been peopled, as English, Scotch, Irish, Dutch, German, etc., each in a shield. On one side of them, Liberty with

18

her pileus (cap), on the other, a rifler in his uniform, with his rifle-gun in one hand and a tomahawk in the other; this dress and these troops with this kind of armor being peculiar to America. . . . Dr. F. proposes a device for a seal: Moses lifting up his wand and dividing the Red Sea, and Pharaoh in his chariot overwhelmed with the waters. This motto, "Rebellion to tyrants is obedience to God."

Mr. Jefferson proposed the children of Israel in the wilderness, led by a cloud by day and a pillar of fire by night; on the other side, Hengist and Horsa, the Saxon chiefs from whom we claim the honor of being descended, and whose political principles and form of government we have assumed. I proposed the choice of Hercules, as engraved by Gribelin, in some editions of Lord Shaftesbury's works. The hero resting on his club. Virtue pointing to her rugged mountain on one hand, and persuading him to ascend. Sloth, glancing at her flowery paths of pleasure, wantonly reclining on the ground, displaying the charms of her eloquence and person, to seduce him into vice. But this is too complicated a group for a seal or medal, and it is not original.[2]

cient symbol probably suggested by Du Simitière, was introduced at the top, and the motto *E PLURIBUS UNUM* across the bottom. This has often been attributed to Jefferson, who wished to express the political concept of powers divided, yet unified as required. However, the motto had appeared on the title page of *The Gentleman's Journal* in London as early as 1692, together with a hand holding a bouquet of flowers (FIGURE 26). It was designed by the editor, Pierre Antoine Motteux, a Huguenot refugee from Rouen. Motteux put a comma after *PLURIBUS,* which, taken with the bouquet, indicates that he may have meant "one chosen from many."[3] The motto became well known to all who read *The Gentleman's Magazine,* as it was called after 1731 and through the period of the Revolution.

Since the motto appeared in one of the

Figure 25

Figure 26

Discussions of these ideas produced various alterations for the obverse, or front of the seal, including substitution of the Goddess of Justice for the American rifleman. The eye of Providence, an an-

best-known periodicals of the day, it was undoubtedly familiar to Jefferson. As early as 1774 he had noted in his almanac: "A proper device (instead of arms) for the American states united would be the Father presenting the bundle of rods to his sons."[4] This referred to the fable of Aesop in which a father called his family of discordant sons about him, and taking a bundle of rods bound together, asked each to break them, which none could do. He then gave each a single rod from the bundle, and these were broken easily.

The reverse of the seal depicted Franklin's suggestion, Pharaoh at the Red Sea, with Jefferson's pillar of fire *in* a cloud at the top. The whole was encircled by Franklin's motto urging rebellion to tyrants, which Jefferson liked so much that he had it cut on his own private seal.

No action was taken on this report; for nearly four years the United States had no coat of arms, and did business without a seal. Then another committee headed by James Lovell of Massachusetts undertook the task and came up with a new design (FIGURE 27). The arms featured a shield

Figure 27

with thirteen diagonal red and white stripes, supported by a warrior on one side and peace bearing an olive branch on the other. Above was a constellation of

Figure 28

thirteen stars, and below, the motto *Bello vel Paci.* The reverse showed a seated figure of Liberty with the line *Virtute Perennis,* and MDCCLXXVI.

Again no action was taken. In May, 1782 still another committee set out to design a seal. One member, Elias Boudinot of South Carolina, probably knew something about numismatics, as he was appointed Director of the Mint at Philadelphia in 1795. This committee called upon William Barton of Philadelphia for advice and creative work. Barton knew heraldry and could sketch. He described in heraldic terms a complicated design (FIGURE 28) introducing a gold helmet and a cock in the crest, and arms displaying an eagle on a Doric column, with as supporters "the Genius of America represented by a Maiden with loose Auburn tresses . . .," and on the other side a man in full armor. Into the composition he also worked a harp, two fleurs-de-lis (to commemorate the French alliance), and a dove, as well as the eye of Providence, thirteen stars and as many stripes. The eagle appears here for the first time, as "emblematical of the Sovereignty of the Government of the United States." In a second version, Barton eliminated the cock and placed the eagle in the crest. The warrior he dressed in Continental uniform, while the harp and fleurs-de-lis were left out. In a scroll was the motto *Virtus sola invicta*. The eye he transferred to the reverse, together with the motto *Deo Favente*. Barton explained the pyramid as signifying "strength and duration."

His design was reported to Congress in May, 1782, but proved unsatisfactory, whereupon it was referred to Charles Thomson, the Secretary of Congress. Thomson had definite and much simpler ideas, which he proceeded to express (FIGURE 29). For the obverse, he specified

Figure 30

Figure 29

the American or bald eagle as the central figure. Peace was to be symbolized by an olive branch in the eagle's right talon, the war power by a bundle of arrows in

the other. The thirteen stars and the constellation were rescued from the second committee's report, while from the report of the first committee he chose the motto *E PLURIBUS UNUM*. For the reverse he accepted Barton's unfinished pyramid and eye, with two new inscriptions, both adapted from Virgil's *Aeneid*;[5] over the eye *ANNUIT COEPTIS* and underneath *NOVUS ORDO SECLORUM*. On the bottom course of the pyramid appeared the year of independence, in Latin numerals.

Thomson's "Device for an Armorial Atchievement"[6] was modified in a few details by Barton, the principal change being substitution of stripes for chevrons on the escutcheon. The seal was adopted by Congress on June 20, 1782 (FIGURE 30).

None of the principal elements of the seal were wholly new. A bundle of thirteen arrows appeared in the North Carolina paper currency of 1775. The olive branch was used on Maryland currency the same year; three years later a fifty dollar bill of that state showed an unfinished pyramid. A Massachusetts copper penny of 1776 depicted thirteen stars surrounding an eagle. The flag had thirteen stripes, and so had the seal of the Board of Admiralty.

The seal was recut in 1841, and altered in disregard of several provisions of law, especially the number of arrows and the width of the stripes. This "illegal" seal was used until attention was drawn to its shortcomings in 1882, when the centennial of the seal was celebrated by the striking of a medal. The reverse had never been cut. In order to do this, and at the same time make the seal "legal," Congress authorized a recutting in 1883. Historical scholars applied themselves to the task, ably aided by Tiffany & Co. The result was a closer adherence to the law as written, in the seal as it appears today. Once more, however, it was decided not to cut the reverse.[7] Need for it had lessened, since pendant seals were no longer used to any extent after 1869. Today the seal, both obverse and reverse, may be most readily examined on the back of the one-dollar bill.

It is interesting to note that in the final seal as approved in 1884 there are thirteen stripes, thirteen stars, thirteen arrows, thirteen olive leaves and thirteen berries, while on the reverse the stones of the pyramid are laid in thirteen courses. The choice of the eagle as the heraldic symbol of the United States was not completely approved by some, including Benjamin Franklin,[8] but has now been sanctified by long use and familiarity. One justification advanced for it has been that the family crest of the Washingtons featured an eagle as far back as 1588.

Another official motto of the United States, *IN GOD WE TRUST,* originated in a quite unofficial manner. In November, 1861, the Rev. M. R. Watkinson of Ridleyville, Pennsylvania, wrote a letter to Salmon P. Chase, Lincoln's Secretary of the Treasury. The Rev. Watkinson was troubled by what seemed to him the godlessness of a nation riven by Civil War. "One fact touching our currency has hitherto been seriously overlooked," he wrote. "I mean the recognition of the Almighty God in some form on our coins. What if our Republic were now shattered beyond reconstruction? Would not the antiquaries of succeeding centuries rightly reason from our past that we were a heathen nation?" He suggested the theme of *God, Liberty, Law,* and asserted, "This would relieve us from the ignominy of heathenism. This would place us openly under the Divine protection we have personally claimed. From my own heart I have felt a national shame in disowning God as not the least of our present national disasters."

Impressed by this plea, Secretary Chase directed that a motto be prepared "expressing in the fewest and tersest words possible this national recognition." Thus *God, our Trust* was cut in the bronze pattern for a ten-dollar gold piece, and soon thereafter another suggestion was considered: *Our Country, Our God.* Secretary Chase himself proposed *In God We Trust,* which made its first appearance on a two-cent coin in 1864. The earlier mottoes on U.S. coins had been such Yankee sayings as "Mind Your Business,"

Figure 31

which appeared on the Fugio cent, first coin issued by the United States.

Today all U.S. fractional currency carries both *IN GOD WE TRUST* and *E PLURIBUS UNUM,* and so does the dollar bill.[9]

Once the nation had won its independence, artists and illustrators made tentative efforts to catch the spirit of the "U. States," as it was generally written. Most of these took the form of Greek goddesses. Sometimes the goddess kept her identifying bonnet of feathers; but seldom was she depicted in the sketchy garb of earlier years. Typical of this period is the British design "An Emblem of America," published in 1798 by John Fairburn (FIGURE 31).

Late in the century came the first stirrings of the Greek revival in architecture and art, strengthening the appeal of the mythological. More and more the female symbol was referred to as Columbia — a name which had been urged by some for

FIRST in WAR,
FIRST in PEACE,
&
FIRST in the Hearts
of his
COUNTRYMEN.

Figure 32

values in which we ardently believe. From our earliest years, her torch has illumined the making of all our policies, both foreign and domestic. A refreshing example from the early 1800's is the painting of Columbia placing a laurel wreath on Washington's head as she steps on the crown (FIGURE 32).

It is interesting to observe how often Miss Columbia (be it noted that she has never lost her virginal status) is called upon to lay down the law to other emblems of our national life, not excepting Uncle Sam himself. Hers is often the voice and hers the flashing eyes which shame the overreaching forces of greed and special privilege. No apostle of misrule can stand against her; she blisters his ears, and will if he persists produce her ancient sword, whereupon, as when the mace appears in Congress, disorder ends and all is tranquil again.

Her lineage, combining as it does the Indian and Greek strains, may help to explain both her fiery temper when provoked and the classic dignity with which she guards the Ark of our Liberties. It is proper that Miss Columbia should do all this, for she is the oldest of our symbolical family still active.

Yankee Doodle, of course, was first of the male line. He was the harum-scarum product of our salad years, the life of many a frontier party — a bumpkin and proud of it — the exact opposite of the mannered, powdered, and furbelowed British with their high-toned notions and superior ways. He began as an object of ridicule. The British officer who laughed at the awkward plowboy riding his work horse into town with a feather in his hat

the nation when the Government had been formed. At first her raiment was a chaste white. But it was only natural that sooner or later, like Britannia, she should be clothed in the national banner. And thus, attired in stars and stripes, the goddess of liberty known as Miss Columbia has continued through the years, representing usually the purer and more idealistic aspects of the American dream. She is the custodian and exemplar of the ultimate

24

all unwittingly launched Yankee Doodle into immortality. For Yankee Doodle was not as slow and backwoodsy as he looked. Quite the contrary: he was brash as a young colt, bright as new paint, and mighty quick on the trigger. After he had proved it at Concord and Bunker Hill, the colonists had a new pride in him and all his raffish doings. They yarned and boasted about his exploits. It made their spines tingle to hear the roll and rumble of the drums of the Continental Line, and "Yankee Doodle" swelling through it clean and clear on the fifes. He was *their* boy, and he was doing all right.

Exactly how it happened is described by the *Pennsylvania Journal* on May 24, 1775, shortly after Lexington and Concord, in its report of those events: "Yesterday, when the second brigade, under Earl Percy, marched out of Boston to reinforce the first, nothing was played by the fifes and drums but Yankee Doodle (which had become their favorite tune ever since that notable exploit, which did so much to honor the troops of Britain's king, of tarring and feathering a poor countryman in Boston, and parading him through the principal streets, under arms, with their bayonets fixed). Upon their return to Boston, one asked his brother officer how he liked the tune now. 'D--n them!' returned he —— 'they made us dance it until we were tired!' Since then Yankee Doodle sounds less sweet in their ears."[10]

The word "Yankee" had been known and used for a long time, especially by foreigners, to denote inhabitants of New England, and by extension, of the country as a whole. Bartlett,[11] quoting a note to the *Poetical Works* of J. Trumbull, says that "the name 'Yankee' was originally given by the Massachusetts Indians to the English colonists, being the nearest sound they could give for 'English.' It was afterwards adopted by the Dutch on the Hudson, who applied the term in contempt to all the people of New England. During the American Revolution, it was eagerly caught at by the British soldiers."

It appears that the Indians pronounced it *Yengees,* to distinguish New Englanders from the Virginians, or Long Knives. In an aside, Bartlett mentions that in New England the word also came to mean a glass of whisky sweetened with molasses, a common beverage in the country.

As for "Yankee Doodle," he says: "In England the air has been traced back to the time of Charles I; and it appears that the doggerel verses that are sung to it can claim nearly as respectable an antiquity." A similar musical theme has also been discovered in the Netherlands, in Hungary, and in Spain. Dr. Richard Shuckburgh, a British Army surgeon during the French and Indian wars, is credited with having composed the lines usually sung, while he was stationed at Fort Crailo, Rensselaer, New York, in 1758. The building where he was billeted is still standing.

In 1814, when the American commissioners arrived in Ghent to negotiate a treaty of peace with Great Britain, musicians in the concert halls of the town sought a suitable balance for "God Save the King." Had the Americans no national airs of their own? At this point Peter, Albert Gallatin's Negro servant, whistled "Hail Columbia," which was at once transposed for the fiddle, and soon be-

Figure 33

came *l'air national des Américains à grand orchestre,* as which it was often played thereafter. When the treaty was signed, however, it is interesting that at the Christmas dinner to which the British commissioners invited the Americans, the air rendered in response to the toast of the President of the United States was "Yankee Doodle."[12] It, as a veteran once remarked of that other anthem, "The Star-Spangled Banner," "had smelled powder smoke."

Yankee Doodle was not a pictorial character, but the mental picture of him generally held was probably not far from that on the cover of the comic weekly named for him (FIGURE 33) which was published for ten months starting in 1846, some years after his heyday. As depicted by Charles Martin, he stands with ax in hand and smoking a "segar." He is surrounded by numerous imps and sprites, while above he is saluted by other creatures of fable, including Harlequin and Don Quixote, as well as Mr. Punch, whose magazine had made its bow in 1841.

3: Yankee Doodle Grows Up

As the nation grew, so did Yankee Doodle. The United States were bursting their buttons, feeling their oats, hankering for bigger and better things. Yankee Doodle didn't quite fit this expansive and industrious time. He was too simple and ingenuous to exemplify the new spirit of the continent-tamers. So Brother Jonathan took over.

In 1848 Bartlett gave the following account of its origin, quoting "a recent number of the *Norwich Courier*," which attributed it to "a gentleman now upwards of eighty years of age, who was an active participator in the scenes of the Revolution." Here is the story:

When George Washington, after having been appointed commander of the army of the Revolutionary War, came to Massachusetts to organize it and made preparations for the defense of the country, he found a great want of ammunition and other means necessary to meet the powerful foe he had to contend with, and great difficulty to obtain them. If attacked in such condition, the cause at once might be hopeless. On one occasion, at that anxious period, a consultation of the officers and others was had, when it seemed no way could be devised to make such preparation as was necessary. His Excellency Jonathan Trumbull the elder was then Governor of the State of Connecticut, on whose judgment and aid the General placed the greatest reliance, and remarked: "We must consult 'Brother Jonathan' on the subject." The General did so, and the Governor was successful in supplying many of the wants of the army. When difficulties afterwards arose, and the army was spread over the country, it became a by-word, *We must consult Brother Jonathan*. The term Yankee is still applied to a portion, but *Brother Jonathan* has now become a designation of the whole country, as John Bull has for England.[1]

27

At first Brother Jonathan was, as Constance Rourke put it, "an out-all-elbows New England country boy with short coatsleeves, shrunken trousers and a blank countenance."[2] Attempts to victimize him were constantly being made by sharpers, who were just as consistently foiled by his native shrewdness. Brother Jonathan was a good deal more serious and mature than Yankee Doodle. Above all he stood for democracy triumphant. He was the American common man, a creature who exemplified the rugged worth of pure character when set against the tawdry pomp of titled and inherited wealth. His essential virtues were common sense and good humor, qualities in which he paid tribute to his fellow citizens and his belief in them.

Jonathan was a common name in England; a London coffeehouse known as Jonathan's had been a place of popular resort by stockjobbers in Queen Anne's time. One possible derivation of the name is from that of John Bull, rather as Peter becomes Peterson in the Scandinavian countries.

Like many another nickname, this one was given at first in derision. In fact, it was not used at all by the pro-American side until after the Revolution. The British, who bestowed it, continued to use the name all through the 1800's, sometimes in pique, sometimes in friendship, generally to represent the typical American rather than Uncle Sam, who came to stand for the U. S. Government.

As early as March 21, 1776, Ezra Stiles wrote from Dighton, Massachusetts: "I saw several gentlemen who came out of Boston last evening. . . . They (the British) left Bunker Hill last Ldsday Morning 17th at Eight o'clock, leaving images of Hay dressed like Sentries standing, with a Label on the Breast of one, inscribed 'Welcome Brother Jonathan.' "[3]

It appears that for a time Yankee Doodle and Jonathan were used almost interchangeably, as in the following verse from the *Royal Gazette,* published in New York, October 3, 1778. Entitled "Yankee Doodle's Expedition to Rhode Island," it consisted of twelve stanzas, of which these are typical:

Begar said Monsieur one grand *Coup*
You shall *bientôt* behold Sir
This was believed as gospel true
And Jonathan *felt bold* Sir.

So Yankee Doodle did forget
The sound of British drum Sir.
How oft it made him quake and sweat
In spite of Yankee Rum, Sir.

As Jonathan so much desir'd,
To shine in martial story,
D'Estaing with politesse retir'd
To leave him all the glory.

On May 27, 1780, reporting a Loyalist attack on Horseneck (now Greenwich), Connecticut, the *Royal Gazette* said:

Last Monday afternoon Col. Delancy with a party of his loyal refugees, made an incursion of about 30 miles into the enemy's country. The foot took post at Byron Bridge, while the horse passed Sherwood's Bridge, and proceeded to Horseneck, where a party of rebels were stationed — they immediately attacked them, killed 8, took prisoners a Lieutenant, a Commissary, a Mr. Knap a Presbyterian Parson, and 36 rank and file, also took and destroyed a piece of cannon, which the Jonathans in vain endeavored to defend; the Loyalists were so quick upon them, that they could not discharge it more than twice before it was taken possession of.

With the end of the Revolution, Jonathan became a sympathetic character adopted by the Americans and accepted by them. He made his first appearance in the flesh on April 16, 1787, and singularly enough, at the John Street Theatre in New York. The occasion was the presentation of a play by Royall Tyler of Boston called *The Contrast*. In it the stage Yankee, who was to be the comedy relief of the American stage for the next century, made his triumphant debut.[4] Jonathan was cast as the servant of Colonel Manly, a hero of the Revolution. In the third act came this scene:

Jenny: So, Mr. Jonathan, I hear you were at the play last night.
Jonathan: At the play! Why, did you think I went to the devil's drawing-room?
Jenny: The devil's drawing-room!
Jonathan: Yes; why ain't cards and dice the devil's device; and the play-house the shop where the devil hangs out the vanities of the world, upon the tenter-hooks of temptation. . . . Oh! no, no, no! You won't catch me at a play-house, I warrant you.
Jenny: Well, Mr. Jonathan, though I don't scruple your veracity, I have some reasons for believing you were there. Pray, where were you about six o'clock?
Jonathan: Why, I went to see one Mr. Morrison, the *hocus-pocus* man; they said as how he could eat a case knife. . . .
Jenny: Well, and did you see the man with his tricks?
Jonathan: Why I vow, as I was looking out for him, they lifted up a great green cloth, and let us look right into the next neighbor's house. Have you a good many houses in New York made so in that 'ere way?
Jenny: Not many: but did you see the family?
Jonathan: Yes, swamp it, I see'd the family. . . .
Jenny: Well, Mr. Jonathan, you were certainly at the play-house.
Jonathan: I at the play-house? Why didn't I see the play then?

Jenny: Why, the people you saw were players.
Jonathan: Mercy on my soul! Did I see the wicked players?

By all accounts the play was a hit. Under date of April 19, 1787, the *New York Journal* ran this review:

On Monday evening . . . was performed at the theatre in this city, amid continued roars of applause, a COMEDY (composed by an American) called the CONTRAST. Novelty, says a correspondent, is ever pleasing: an American comic production is a novelty — therefore it was pleasing. . . . The striking Contrast, in this piece, is between a person who had made his tour of Europe, studied the *bon ton,* with his galloned attendant . . . and an heroic, sentimental American Colonel, with his honest waiting-man.

Thereafter the references to Jonathan in the public prints are quite frequent. About 1804 there appeared "The Embargo, a New Song" of which the following is one typical stanza:

Then Jonathan and I went down
To look around the wharf Sir,
And there we see a hundred men
Shoving a big boat off Sir.

Yankee Doodle Keep it up,
Yankee Doodle Dandy,
We'll soak our hides in home made rum
If we can't get French brandy.

Another in the same vein came in 1806 with the publication in Philadelphia of "The Country Lovers, or Mr. Jonathan Jolthead's Courtship with Miss Sally Snapper: An Excellent New Song, said to have been written by its Author, and really founded on fact."
A year later in New York was issued

Figure 34

Jonathan Postfree, or the Honest Yankee. A Musical farce. In three acts. However, there is no record that this piece was ever played.

The earliest description of Jonathan was set down by James K. Paulding in his book *The Diverting History of John Bull and Brother Jonathan,* published in 1812:

At the time this story opens, Bull's family had got to be so numerous that his farm was hardly large enough to portion them all with; so he sent his younger son, Jonathan, or as he was familiarly called *Brother Jonathan,* to settle some new lands which he had on the other side of the mill-pond. . . . In a little time Jonathan grew up to be very large for his age; and became a tall, stout, double-jointed, broad-footed cub of a fellow, awkward in his gait, and simple in his appearance; but showing a lively, shrewd look, and having the promise of great strength when he should get his full growth. He was rather an odd looking chap, in truth, and had many queer ways; but everybody that had seen John Bull, saw a great likeness between them, and swore that he was John's own boy, and a true chip of the old block. Like the old Squire, he was apt to be blustering and saucy, but in the main was a peaceable

sort of careless fellow, that would quarrel with nobody if you would only let him alone. He used to dress in homespun trousers with a huge bagging seat, which seemed to have nothing in it. This made people to say he had no *bottom;* but whoever said so lied, as they found to their cost, whenever they put Jonathan in a passion. He always wore a short Linsey-woolsey coat, that did not cover above half his breech, and the sleeves of which were so short that his hand and wrist came out beyond them, looking like a shoulder of mutton. All of which was in consequence of his growing so fast that he outgrew his clothes.

Paulding was an American writer and politician, of Dutch descent. He was a friend of Washington Irving and sometimes collaborated with him. He served as Secretary of the Navy in the cabinet of President Van Buren.

Brother Jonathan figures in the cartoons which illustrated the third edition of Paulding's book, published in 1827. One of these, a take-off on the Boston Tea Party (FIGURE 34), shows "Jonathan throwing the Tea-Kettle at Bull's Head." This spirited work was probably

Figure 35

by S. Kennedy, who had been a partner of the noted William Charles.

Of interest from this period is Amos Doolittle's cartoon (FIGURE 35) "Brother Jonathan Administering a Salutary Cordial to John Bull." This was published shortly after Commodore Oliver Hazard Perry's victory on Lake Erie in 1813, a feat in which the American engravers visibly rejoiced. In a letter offering this print for sale, Doolittle wrote: "Although many caricatures extant are of no use, and some of them have an immoral effect, I flatter myself that this will not answer that description. At the present time, it is believed, it will have a tendency to inspire our countrymen with confidence in themselves, and eradicate any terrors that they may feel as respects the enemy they have to combat." Doolittle, who lived in New Haven, Connecticut, had also published in 1775 four rough but well-known engravings of the battle of Lexington.

In 1820 the British writer Sydney Smith commented as follows:

David Porter and Stephen Decatur are very brave men; but they will prove an unspeakable misfortune to their country, if they influence Jonathan into a love of naval glory, and inspire him to any other love of war than that which is founded upon a determination not to submit to serious insult and injury.

We can inform Jonathan what are the inevitable consequences of being too fond of glory; — taxes upon every article which enters into the mouth, or covers the back, or is placed under the foot — taxes upon everything which it is pleasant to see, hear, feel, smell, or taste — taxes upon warmth, light and locomotion — taxes on everything on earth, and the waters under the earth.

In 1848, James Russell Lowell made this observation:

. . . Yet, after all, thin, speculative Jonathan is more like the Englishman of two centuries ago than John Bull himself is. He has lost somewhat in solidity, has become fluent

Figure 36

A popular weekly journal of the day bore Jonathan's name. The *Brother Jonathan* was, according to a contemporary notice, "embellished with highly finished and spirited engravings — each number contains a popular piece of music, and comprises thirty-two pages of reading matter printed on fine white paper, and in handsome clear type."

Jonathan is often depicted as whittling, a pastime which was once universally enjoyed in America. While Sam Houston was a U. S. senator he liked to whittle wooden hearts and send them up to pretty girls in the Senate galleries. Longstreet whittled to rest his jangled nerves after Pickett's charge at Gettysburg. Grant whittled while meditating a bold stroke in the Wilderness. Somehow an American with a knife just naturally had to use it, especially in moments of tedium or stress.

Though it reflected some of his attributes, the South never came to identify itself with Brother Jonathan to any degree. Indeed, when South Carolina seceded from the Union late in 1860, there appeared in a Confederate journal a poem entitled "Caroline's Farewell to Brother Jonathan."[5] It said in part:

> Farewell, we must part, we have turned
> from the land,
> Of our cold-hearted brother with tyran-
> nous hand,
> Who assumed all our rights as a favor
> to grant,
> And whose smile ever covered the sting
> of a taunt.

And in a warming vein of recollection . . .

> O Jonathan, Jonathan, vassal of pelf,
> Self-righteous, self-glorious, yes, every
> inch self,

and adaptable, but more of the original groundwork of character remains. . . . John Bull has suffered the idea of the Invisible to be very much fattened out of him. Jonathan is conscious still that he lives in a world of the Unseen as well as the Seen. To move John you must make your fulcrum of solid beef and pudding; an abstract idea will do for Jonathan.

Jonathan's progress is illustrated by his likeness on the front cover of the January, 1852, edition of *Yankee Notions* (FIGURE 36), an illustrated weekly published by Thomas W. Strong. Himself a general illustrator, Strong also published the work of many others. This particular drawing was by Augustus Hoppin.

Your loyalty now, is all bluster and
    boast —
But was dumb when the foemen in-
    vaded our coast.

The final jibe refers to the lack of enthusiasm in New England for the War of
1812, which culminated in the Hartford
Convention with its own talk of secession.

That the sections had other differences
on our national symbols is demonstrated
by Thomas Crawford's nineteen-foot figure of Freedom which tops the Capitol in
Washington. A great crowd assembled on
December 2, 1863, to see this crowning
touch put in place. At noon a battery of
field guns fired the national salute, and the
Capitol was complete in its present form.
It is ironic that the statue was designed
while Jefferson Davis was Secretary of
War and in charge of the construction of
the Capitol. Davis would not allow Crawford to use the Phrygian or liberty cap on
his statue because it had been the symbol
of liberated slaves in Rome and elsewhere
through the centuries. Hence Crawford
substituted a crested helmet, and so it is
today (FIGURE 37).

Jonathan did yeoman service during the
Civil War; hence it is rather surprising to
find Colonel James F. Rusling declaring
in 1865 in the *United Service Magazine*
that he had outlived his usefulness:

Brother Jonathan is dead. Born in another
age, and of the day of small things, he has
passed away. His name, even, bids fair to become a myth among the people. He expired
with the sound of the first gun fired *from*
South Carolina *against* Fort Sumter, and in
his stead, there stands the game-cock, W. T.
Sherman. The old time beaver, the high
collar and big cravat, the long-tailed coat,
abbreviated breeches, cowhide boots, and
"cute individual" from "way down East" —

Figure 37

all these have passed into history, and today
the true representative American is the
Union Soldier. Yankee Doodle is decidedly
looking up.

Colonel Rusling's obsequies proved to
be somewhat premature. Brother Jonathan was still alive and kicking; he was
due for many another appearance, both
here and abroad, especially in the pages
of *Punch*, which seemed to be particularly fond of him.

4: A Matter of Pride

We have seen how Pocahontas grew into Columbia, and Yankee Doodle into Brother Jonathan, both developments reflecting the growth of the American spirit and the deepening sense of nationhood. But America was to find its truest expression in the new Uncle Sam symbol.

It was the War of 1812 that evoked Uncle Sam. Perhaps he came into being because he was needed to symbolize the yearnings of the new nation for fulfillment. These were crystallized in one place, at one time. References to Uncle Sam began in 1813 and thereafter became increasingly numerous. He derived from a man who lived through those troublous times — meat packer Samuel Wilson of Troy, New York.

The emergence of the Uncle Sam image in 1813 coincided exactly with the vigorous reassertion of American rights. But even more importantly, it provided a rallying point for citizens of the various states whose pride had been injured by the cavalier attitude of Europe toward the new Republic. With no hereditary monarch to symbolize the nation, and to centralize its loyalties, some such image was bound to come.

Like most young nations, the United States of the early 1800's suffered from a gnawing inferiority complex. On occasion this sense of inadequacy evoked reactions out of all proportion to the challenge. Jonathan had taken over a job that was proving to be bigger than he had suspected. He was nervous, and his voice was changing. Sometimes when he wanted to roar like a lion, what came out was more like the bleat of a lamb. The core of the trouble lay in the weakness of the Federal Government. In September, 1813,

Figure 38

a pitched battle was fought between "Uncle Sam's Men" and the "Men of New York," over who should collect duties at the Canadian border. Militia enlistments were short and apparently in some cases at the pleasure of the recruit. Boston's *Columbian Centinel* for October 9, 1813, carried a dispatch from Burlington, Vermont, as follows:

The patriotic volunteers, who have *marched* here to guard the public stores in the absence of the regular army, are taking "long furloughs" and volunteering for *home* by tens and fifties and hundreds. The pretense is, that Uncle Sam, the now popular explication of the U. S., does not pay well, and that the cold begins to pinch.[1]

Much of the action took place on the northern frontier. The U. S. Government had purchased three hundred acres at Greenbush, just south of Troy, and erected there a number of large barrack buildings, twelve of them around a parade ground and several others on a nearby eminence. These provided accommodations for over six thousand troops. Thereafter infantry and artillery columns moved often through Troy on their way to camp. Troy's own contingents included the Troy Fusileers, the Trojan Greens, and the Troy Invincibles (FIGURE 38).[2] Here throughout the war the troops came to rest and recuperate from the rigors of northern campaign-

35

ing, and here they always found the big casks marked "U. S." filled with the salt beef and pork which in those days were the mainstay of the Army cook.

Troy in the early 1800's was a bustling town with high hopes for a prosperous future. Its native Dutch conservatism had been mixed with the enterprise of immigrants from New England, most of them from beyond the Green Mountains, and all bent on finding new homes and better ways of making a living. Among this outflow had been the brothers Samuel and Ebenezer Wilson (or "Willson," as they spelled it in those early years).

It was an era of strong political feeling. As Troy historian John Woodworth writes:

At this Time a Spirit of Intolerance existed, beyond the Control of sober men, of either Party; there were more than the ordinary Causes for this; the influence of the French Revolution upon this Country was great; the Annunciation of Liberty restored in *France,* after a dark night of Centuries, gave an Impulse, that caused Delirium in the public Mind, especially among the Masses. It was enough that the Chain was broken, and the Bastile destroyed; the *Marsellais Hymn* and Ça Ira, were chaunted in our Streets, scarce a Thought occurred, whether here were Materials to lay the Foundation of Rational Liberty.[3]

Even so, Troy was a convivial town. Much of the social life centered about the taverns, of which there were more than a dozen. Ashley's, the first and biggest, allured the passer-by on River Street with a rotating signboard. Rules of the Hart, kept by Moses Craft, specified: "No profane language, no fighting or threatenings; no gambling, which is the foundation of the above profanities. Horses kept for three shillings a night per span." Bellmen cried the news and the mail was brought by postriders. With many veterans of the Revolution living in Troy, July Fourth was celebrated by parades and prayer meetings. Bands of Indians sometimes wandered through the town, and as late as 1806 several of the Stockbridge tribe alarmed the citizens by staging a brawl on one of the main streets.

There was a great deal of social drinking, and no dinner party was complete without a series of toasts. Dipped tallow candles served for illumination, often in sconces. Dwellings were plainly furnished, with broad floor boards, generally uncarpeted except for a few scatter rugs. Beds were usually four-posters and canopied, with big feather mattresses and patchwork quilts, the whole rising to such a height that one retired by climbing a ladder. Dinner was the big meal of the day and was served at noon. Most men came home from work to dine and often took a short nap afterward. Grace was said both before and after meals, in a standing position. The customary drink was bohea tea made strong in a black earthenware pot. Aesthetes sometimes took tea by holding loaf sugar in the mouth and allowing the tea to pass through it. For dessert there had to be at least four kinds of cake and preserves. Meals were enjoyed in the leisurely fashion that promotes good digestion. There still prevailed the elaborate eighteenth-century manners which required that letters begin with "Honoured Sir" or "Respected Madam" and close with "Your Most Obedient and Humble Servant," or "Yours Ever to Command."

The headquarters of General Henry Dearborn, Greenbush soon became a principal focus of American operations in the north. And it fell to the lot of Samuel Wilson to provision the troops stationed at this camp. He and the General had this in common: they had both grown up in New Hampshire and both were Democrats. The General was a man of mark; he had served from Bunker Hill to Yorktown and had been Secretary of War for eight years under Jefferson.

At Greenbush as elsewhere, Troy historian Arthur James Weise tells us, Samuel found making friends as easy as breathing. "Being one of the first settlers, and besides having a kind and benevolent disposition, he won the esteem and affection of everybody . . . and was more generally designated as Uncle Sam than by his proper name."[4]

It was an era which was to produce many other sobriquets. Americans have always given nicknames to those about whom they have felt strongly. There was "Old Hickory" (Andrew Jackson); soon they were to call General Winfield Scott "Old Fuss and Feathers," General Zachary Taylor "Old Rough and Ready," General William Henry Harrison "Tippecanoe," and Martin Van Buren "Matty of Kinderhook."

Hence it was probably natural that some such cognomen should settle upon so well-known and widely respected a citizen as Samuel Wilson. Samuel came by his naturally. His brothers and sisters raised such large families that he accumulated scores of nephews and nieces. There is a story that when one of the Wilson sons strayed from home and was asked where he lived, he identified himself as "Uncle Sam's boy," whereupon he was returned home forthwith.

It is certain, therefore, that Uncle Sam was so called by his many friends up and down the Hudson Valley quite some time before the outbreak of the War of 1812, which was to give the name its larger significance.

37

5: The Legend Is Born

Some will wonder why it was that the Uncle Sam story began during a war so much smaller than the mighty conflicts that have raged in the century since then, and in — of all places — a meat-packing yard. But great events often have humble beginnings.

Samuel Wilson and his brother had advertised as early as 1805 that they could butcher and pack 150 head of cattle per day (FIGURE 39). The firm was known as E. & S. Wilson. They also made casks in which they packed the salted meat, and dealt in salt on the side. Hence, when war came, they were in a good position to bid for Government contracts. Samuel not only supplied meat to the military on his own, he secured an appointment as inspector of beef and pork for the northern Army. In this capacity he inspected meat packed for the account of Elbert Ander-son, who had a contract to supply the six thousand troops encamped at nearby Greenbush. The records show that Secretary of War Eustis contracted with Elbert Anderson, Jr., of New York City, to supply and issue all rations required by the U. S. troops in New York and New Jersey for one year. Accordingly, Anderson advertised on October 6, 13, and 20, 1812, for sealed bids on two thousand barrels of prime pork and three thousand barrels of prime beef, to be packed in full-bound barrels of white oak (FIGURE 40). Ebenezer and Samuel Wilson furnished provisions under this contract.[1]

What happened then is best told by one who was apparently on the spot when Uncle Sam's name was conferred upon the Government itself. His story appeared in the New York *Gazette* of May 12, 1830, shortly after Elbert Anderson's

SLAUGHTERING & PACKING.

THE undersigned having two large and convenient SLAUGHTER-HOUSES, beg leave to acquaint their customers, and others, that they will be enabled to *kill, cut* and *pack* 150 head of Cattle per day ; and, from their local situation, pledge themselves to accommodate those who may favour them with a call, on terms as low as can be obtained in the State.

They have on hand a large supply of BARRELS and SALT, which will be disposed of on the lowest terms.

All those who shall be under the necessity of waiting 24 hours for their cattle to be slaughtered, shall have them pastured free of expence.   *E. & S. WILSON.*
Troy, September 17, 1805.

Figure 39

PROPOSALS
FOR BEEF AND PORK.

SEALED Proposals will be received through the medium of the Post-Offices at Albany and New-York, directed to the subscriber, until the 25th of October, for 2000 barrels PRIME PORK, and 3000 barrels PRIME BEEF, to be delivered in the months of January, February, March and April, at Waterford, Troy, Albany and New-York. The whole to be put up in *full bound barrels* of white oak. No proposals need be offered for less than one hundred barrels. Twenty per cent will be paid in advance at the time of executing the contract 20 per cent on the first day of January, and 20 per cent the first day of March, the remainder on the first day of May, 1813. The Contractor reserves to himself the privilege of choosing his inspector in the counties the provisions are put up in: The preference will be given to those whose reputation and security will insure the faithful compliance of the terms of the contract.
ELBERT ANDERSON, Jun.
October 1st, 1812.   *Army Contractor.*

Figure 40

Figure 41 (below)

death, which occurred on April 17 of that year. This eyewitness story was captioned "A Neat Communication — Origin of 'Uncle Sam.' " It recounted the beginning of the "Uncle Sam" legend and Anderson's connection with it as follows:

Much learning and research have been exercised in tracing the origin of odd names and odd sayings, which taking their rise in some trifling occurrence or event, easily explained or well understood for a time, yet, in the course of years, becoming involved in mystery, assume an importance equal at least to the skill and ingenuity required to explain or trace them to their origin. "The Swan with two necks," "the Bull and Mouth," "All my Eye, Betty Martin," and many others, are of this character — and who knows but, an hundred years hence, some "learned commentator" may puzzle his brain to furnish some ingenious explanation of the origin of the national appellation placed at the head of this article. To aid him, therefore, in this research, I will state the facts as they occurred under my own eyes.

Immediately after the declaration of the last war with England, Elbert Anderson, of New York, a contractor, visited Troy on the Hudson, where was concentrated, and where he purchased, a large quantity of provisions — beef, pork, etc. The inspectors of these

UNCLE SAM WILSON OF TROY SUPPLIED BEEF TO THE UNITED STATES ARMY DURING THE WAR OF 1812 — STAMPING HIS BARRELS WITH THE LETTERS 'U.S.' THIS BEEF BECAME KNOWN TO THE ARMY AS *UNCLE SAMS* AND THIS FAMILIAR APPELLATION WAS THEREAFTER BESTOWED ON OUR OWN GOVERNMENT

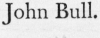
DOLL,
the Landlady.

Kill him Bona, kill him, 'tis what we're all after.

Drive the business Split-foot, it's an ill wind that blows nobody down.

Split-Foot.

Doll, we'll win any way.
Kill him Bona, I want to smoke him eternally.

Bonapart.

Johnny, Master's coming.

You old tyrant, I'll hew you to pieces before my Master.

You little Corsican Sergeant, I'll put you into my snuff box.

John Bull.

Since money is plenty and millions are lending,
If I get a few shillings pray don't be off, nurd,
I love to see soldiers repair to the northward,
And teamsters transporting their stores from the southward.

There's good pay by the month, and abundance of rations,
Which keeps up the money in good circulation,
I have excellent flum, wont you come in and smoke?
(Now this is put in for to humor the joke.)

Since Cain was a boy I've delighted in fighting,
And to further the business my scribes are now writing,
And since we've got Bona & Johnny together,
I want he'd do with him as Cain with his brother:
For since he's got old, he is not worth keeping,
And I want him below, where I'll keep him from sleeping;
Then add this new service unto the old score,
And I'll pay altogether when time is no more.

My name it is Bona, the terror of nations,
Give Quebec up to James, or I'll hew you to pieces,
This makes me to laugh like a man that is frantic,
For then I'll be able to cross the Atlantic.
If uncle Sam needs, I'd be glad to assist him,
For it makes my heart bleed we live at such a distance,
If he calls me to Quebec, I'll lead on the van,
And for Johnny Bull we'll not leave him a man.

My name is John Bull, it strikes Bona like thunder,
If I meet with old Rodgers, I'll make him to wonder.
He talks of his ship being swift in her motion,
But I'll let him know I am king on the ocean.
My old British subjects who claim his protection,
I want to take home to the house of correction,
If the right to search him is the question in full,
I'll stick to that text while my name is JOHN BULL.

---

articles at that place were Messrs. Ebenezer and Samuel Wilson. The latter gentleman (invariably known as "Uncle Sam") generally superintended in person a large number of workmen, who, on this occasion, were employed in overhauling the provisions purchased by the contractor for the Army. The casks were marked E. A. — U. S. This work fell to the lot of a facetious fellow in the employ of the Messrs. Wilson, who, on being asked by some of his fellow-workmen the meaning of the mark (for the letters U. S., for United States, were almost entirely new to them) said that he did not know unless it meant Elbert Anderson and Uncle Sam — alluding exclusively then, to the said "Uncle Sam" Wilson. The joke took among the workmen, passed currently and, "Uncle Sam" himself being present, was occasional-

ly rallied by them on the increasing extent of his possessions.

Many of these workmen being of a character denominated "food for powder," were found shortly after following the recruiting drum, and pushing toward the frontier lines, for the double purpose of meeting the enemy, and eating the provisions they had lately labored to put in good order. Their old jokes of course accompanied them, and before the first campaign ended, this identical one first appeared in print — it gained favor rapidly, till it penetrated and was recognized in every part of the country, and will no doubt continue to while the United States remains a nation. It originated precisely as above stated; and the writer of this article distinctly recollects remarking, at the time when it first appeared in print, to a person

40

A View of the Northern Expedition in Miniature.

James War. Tom Patriot. John Adams. John Rogers.

Kill him Bona, kill him & I'll take Canada.

Here comes No. 1. Let me at him Bona & I'll take him down

Kill him Bona, & I'll pay all damages.

Let me at him Bona, and I'll blow him to atoms.

Columbia, Columbia, to glory arise,
Fly quick to the north, make Canada a prize,
While it's mine to command, it is your's to obey,
Then all hands make ready to seize on the prey.
We'll repair to the northward, stick close by the lines,
Lest we get too far in those northerly climes,
When the winter sets in, to Greenbush we'll retire,
And smoak our long pipes by the side of the fire.

Starvation's the fate of the British empire,
My destructive machine will soon make them expire,
Methinks I will make them come under my thumb,
With my little bark that mounts only one gun,
I will bring them to terms by the force of this measure,
Then we'll go abroad & return home at pleasure,
We'll sail to sweet France, & in ev'ry direction,
And no British tyrant demand our protection.

My name is Taxation—in my introduction,
Some people I vext, to prevent their destruction,
Had I in the place of some others been sitting,
I'd built me a navy to cope with Great Britain.
But now I'm retir'd, sees the states in a bustle,
And all I'm afraid, paid too dear for the whistle,
One caution I'd give you before that I leave you,
I'd send Barlow to Bona, and borrow a navy.

My fleet to John Bull no true homage will pay,
Though his orders in council forever should stay;
He talks of a right for to search for his slaves,
Before I grant that I shall sink in the waves:
He had better be silent and send me no threat,
Les I catch his fish in my old yankee net,
He builds on the Indians that's now with him,
But if Uncle Sam lives, they will all be Burgoyn'd.

Figure 42

who was equally aware of its origin, how odd it would be should this silly joke, originating in the midst of beef, pork, pickle, mud, salt and hoop-poles, eventually become a national cognomen.

Everybody around Troy knew Uncle Sam, hence the speed with which the reference caught on. In a short time all Government property was being referred to as Uncle Sam's — wagons, arms, payrolls, and the like (FIGURE 41). The periodicals of 1814 are full of references to the term. In a way this matches the use and popularity of "G. I." (for "government issue") during World War II to mean everything connected with the armed services, including the men themselves.

The earliest use of the term "Uncle Sam" in this connection which has been discovered thus far was in a broadside reproduced herewith (FIGURE 42), which gives evidence of having been printed in the spring of 1813.

Under the crude woodcuts are two mentions of Uncle Sam. One is in doggerel under the cartoon of "Bonapart": "If Uncle Sam needs, I'll be glad to assist him." The other appears in the last line of the similar caption under John Rodgers[2]: "But if Uncle Sam lives, they will all be Burgoyn'd." This refers back, of course,

Figure 43

to the Revolutionary victory over that British general.

The broadside can be dated in part by the account of the battle of Queenston, which took place on October 20, 1812. On the opposite page, under "John Bull in a Pet," are references to British ships defeated by the U. S. Navy, including the *Guerrière, Macedonian, Java, Frolic,* and *Peacock.* Of these the last chronologically was the *Peacock,* which was taken February 24, 1813. The "Northern Expedition" then in preparation was General Dearborn's campaign against the British posts along the northern shore of Lake Ontario, which got under way early in the spring of 1813. It would appear, therefore, that this broadside dates from about March of that year. The characters depicted are, left to right, Dolly Madison, the Devil, Bonaparte, John Bull, James Madison, Thomas Jefferson, John Adams, and Commodore John Rodgers.

The original of the broadside is in the Library of Congress. Its significance was discovered by Frederick R. Goff, Chief of the Rare Book Division, who believes that it was printed in northern New York, possibly Troy or Albany.

The next reference, which for many years was taken as the first, appeared in the Troy *Post* for September 7, 1813 (FIGURE 43). If this article is any indication, the name seems to have been first employed by editors opposed to the Government and "Mr. Madison's War." Doubtless few who used it knew how it had started. In any case, the political bias, if any, was soon forgotten. The whole thing savors of a wry joke — one which grew so fast that it outran its locale and assumed a significance of which its originators had never dreamed. The article begins as follows:

FOR THE TROY POST

"Loss upon loss, and no ill luck stirring but what lights upon UNCLE SAM'S* shoulders," exclaim the Government Editors, in every part of the country. . . .

[The asterisk refers to a note at the end of the piece:] *This cant name for our government has got almost as current as "John Bull." The letters U. S. on the government waggons, etc. are supposed to have given rise to it.*

Though references to Uncle Sam multiplied daily, there is no written or printed evidence connecting Samuel Wilson with the Government's new nickname for another seventeen years. The derivation remained a simple Hudson Valley folk tale for all that time, passed on by word of mouth, and considered as of only passing interest. But it was recalled years later by men who had lived through those times, and who had seen and heard the beginnings of the new national character.

Most revealing is the testimony of the late Lucius E. Wilson of New York City, given in 1917 when he was eighty-one years of age. Mr. Wilson was one of Uncle Sam's authentic great-nephews. He said:

I was about 18 when Uncle Sam passed away. He was the old original Uncle Sam that gave the name to the United States. . . . Uncle Sam Wilson engaged in many enterprises, employed many hands, had extensive acquaintance, was jolly, genial, generous, and known and called "Uncle Sam" by everyone. His wife was like him, widely known and called "Aunt Betsey." In my boyhood days I lived within half a dozen blocks of Uncle Sam. When a boy my father told me the Uncle Sam story and I have heard him tell it to others dozens of times.

After my grandfather, Edward Wilson's death, near Ballston in 1843, grandmother came to Troy and lived directly opposite Uncle Sam's on the northeast corner of Ferry and Seventh streets. I went there often and could see Uncle Sam (across the street) sitting on his porch. He played a mean joke on me once. Sent to take a pail of soup to Grandma, I stopped first to see him and when I delivered the pail to Grandmother it contained nothing but water which he had substituted. Uncle Sam enjoyed the joke but Grandma called him "an old trickster."

Lucius Wilson ascribes the origin of the Uncle Sam story to an Irish watchman. He says that on one occasion when a large consignment of casks and packages were awaiting shipment on a dock, each marked with a large "E.A.-U.S.," a party of visitors landed there and on seeing the pile of freight, inquired who owned it. The Irishman replied that it belonged to Mr. Anderson and Uncle Sam. "Uncle Sam who?" he was asked.

"Why, Uncle Sam Wilson. It is he who is feeding the army."

This, he tells us, was considered a huge joke and quickly spread. In the army the soldiers called the beef and pork Uncle Sam's and said that Uncle Sam was caring for them. And thus the joke spread throughout the land.[3]

What did Uncle Sam look like? Lucius Wilson continues:

In form and carriage he greatly resembled Abraham Lincoln. He was tall, well preserved and the type of the well-to-do old gentleman of his day. Had high cheek bones, was clean shaven and wore his grey hair rather long.[4]

Another descendant was William Henry Jackson, the noted photographer of the old West. Mr. Jackson published his autobiography *Time Exposure* in 1940, and in it he set down his recollections of his ancestor.

Quite the most distinguished member of my family was a great-uncle of my mother's (Harriet Maria Allen). He enjoyed during his later years a singular fame that has hardly diminished today — a fame that no other American has quite equalled. That is an extravagant claim, but I believe no one will refuse the honor to the man who has personified his country for a century and a quarter.

After recounting the story, he mentions the contribution of Thomas Nast, and continues:

In the 80's when I met Nast in Colorado he learned for the first time that "Uncle Sam" had a flesh-and-blood prototype in my great-great-Uncle. Uncle Sam was to pay quite a price for his distinction: for forty years simple people, as well as many not so simple, pestered him to set them up in business or, in the very least, to supply them with farms. . . . Samuel Wilson came of tough stock. He lived until 1854, when I was eleven. . . .

Several years later young Jackson started to paint in oils, and

began to copy old portraits. I completed a family gallery, including a likeness of Samuel Wilson. If that one should ever turn up again, I am sure that no one would ever recognize "Uncle Sam," for my portrait

The hat was high and bell-crowned, of felted fur; the collar of the shirt high and connected with it, the bosom frilled, projecting well out, with a jeweled pin or brooch in it; cravat white and very wide, stiffened with what was termed a "pudding." Waistcoat single-breasted, buff cloth, with gold or gilt buttons. . . . Coat blue, swallow-tailed, with high, rolling collar and a lapel of peculiar shape, and very high waisted, showing the waistcoat underneath it. Pantaloons close fitting, with an arrow fall in front, and fitted below the knee for the wearing of boots outside, with a tassel in front. Watch carried in a fob in the pantaloons and attached to a ribbon with a seal suspended to it. In the Spring and Autumn, in place of an overcoat, a spencer or jacket was worn over the coat. . . .

The anachronisms of the (Uncle Sam) figure as universally given are many: thus colored skirts were not known until about 1829, and striped pantaloons were of a later date, and straps under the boots did not appear until about 1825, and they were a part of the pantaloons fashioned over the boot in front and buttoned under it, and known as "à la mode de Paris," and a goatee or imperial was not worn until very late in the thirties. Colored shirts came in about 1828. The goatee preceded by a few years the imperial, introduced by Napoleon III.

As late as 1838, George K. Glidden, Consul in Egypt, appeared on Broadway wearing a full mustache and people stared at him as if he were a wild man.[5]

Figure 44

showed him without the characteristic whiskers. Uncle Sam never wore them while I knew him. . . .

How did the real Uncle Sam dress? Charles H. Haswell, a veteran mining engineer who had lived through the era that produced Uncle Sam, wrote in 1899, when he was ninety-two years old, a description of Uncle Sam's proper costume (FIGURE 44).

Mr. Haswell also guided an artist in drawing an accurate picture of the figure which he had described. The face he chose was that of Henry Clay, a bit of irony when one considers the lifelong attachment of Samuel Wilson to Andrew Jackson.

From the foregoing it would appear that the vestments of the Uncle Sam figure so familiar today trace back more to those of the thirties when the first cartoons appeared, than to the War of 1812.

6: A Man Called Uncle Sam

To most people it still comes as news that Uncle Sam really lived, and that his nickname, together with a good many of his personal attributes, were transferred to the new symbol of the United States during his lifetime.

The original of Uncle Sam didn't seek the honor, though he certainly knew that it had been bestowed upon him. Indeed, it is something of a tribute to him that he never sought to capitalize upon his renown, except by being a good citizen.

Uncle Sam was born Samuel Wilson in Menotomy (later West Cambridge and now Arlington), Massachusetts, on September 13, 1766,[1] and was baptized the next day. He was the seventh in a family of thirteen children. Two died in infancy; nine sons and two daughters survived. The Wilson property was located in the triangle formed by Massachusetts Avenue, Mystic Street and Russell Street, now bisected by the little-used line of the Boston & Maine Railroad. Title traces back to Robert Wilson, who bought it from John Brown of Marlborough, Massachusetts, on October 27, 1665. Robert Wilson[2] is believed to have come over from Scotland.

Old maps show Fowle's Pond just north of the Wilson site and south of Summer Street. This has now been filled in, but a large open field shows where it was, and at the eastern end one can still find the flowing sluiceways of the old Fowle's Mill. The bridge over this brook on the Woburn Road was known as Wilson's Bridge as late as 1850. Samuel A. Fowle's land had been bought from the Cutter family, and the Wilson line is mentioned on Cutter deeds of 1686, 1725, and 1768.

Samuel's father, Edward Wilson, married Lucy Francis of Medford on November 23, 1758. Edward "owned the covenant" at the Congregational Precinct Church on October 21, 1759. The records show that Edward Wilson improved the land of the heirs of Andrew Wilson, deceased, in 1770 and 1778. Whether these were houses or barns is not stated.

The property has been researched by Miss Elizabeth Orton Jones, the well-known artist, who believes that the site of the Wilson home was about where the station now stands, and an inspection of the area reinforces this conclusion.[3] It requires little effort of the imagination to follow young Sam Wilson over the paths between Fowle's Mill and the Boston Road (now Massachusetts Avenue) along which he must have scampered many a time.

Samuel was going on nine years old on the night of the eighteenth of April, 1775, when Paul Revere rode out from Boston, down the Medford Road and right past the Wilson place toward Lexington, warning of the British march to Concord. Next day a British convoy of supplies in charge of a sergeant's guard, forming part of Lord Percy's reinforcements for the force which had marched out so blithely that morning, took a wrong turn and became separated from the main body. What happened then is recounted on a tablet in front of what was then the Congregational Church:

AT THIS POINT
APRIL 19, 1775
THE OLD MEN OF MENOTOMY
CAPTURED A CONVOY OF
EIGHTEEN SOLDIERS
WITH SUPPLIES ON THE WAY TO
JOIN THE BRITISH AT LEXINGTON

There were only twelve of these old men, but some had been soldiers in the French war, and they knew how to handle a firelock. At their first volley several of the guards fell; the rest, with the drivers, ran toward Spy Pond, into which they threw their arms. Nearby they met an old woman known as Mother Batherick, who was digging dandelions, and to her they surrendered. Before turning them over to the minutemen she said to them: "If you ever live to get back, you tell King George that an old woman took six of his grenadiers prisoners!" So it was that the first prisoners of the Revolution were taken in Menotomy, and by a grandmother. The incident was caught up scornfully by the opposition papers in England, which asked: "If one old Yankee woman can take six grenadiers, how many soldiers will it require to conquer America?"

Meanwhile the townspeople had drawn the British wagons onto the Wilson land and down into the hollow, just northeast of where the railroad station now stands, to keep them out of sight. There some of the wagons upset, and the soldiers' packs and blankets were shared by all comers. The horses which were killed in the first fusillade were dragged to Spring Valley, near Spy Pond, to get them out of sight, and here the bones lay whitening for years.

The British column returning from Concord had been hotly engaged all the way. They met their reinforcements near Lexington, which formed a hollow square as some protection from the galling fire. An officer said: "They lay down on the ground, with their tongues hanging from their mouths, like dogs after a chase."[4]

Figure 45

Amos Doolittle drew a series of sketches illustrating the action of that day, which were published in December, 1775. In one, British Lt. Colonel Francis Smith and Major John Pitcairn (with telescope) are shown surveying the rebel position on East Hill in Concord (FIGURE 45).

It was about an hour's march from Lexington back to Menotomy. The route descended into the long main street of the village. There some eighteen hundred rebels were waiting, Edward Wilson among them. The clash that ensued was the bloodiest of the day. Fighting raged house-to-house. The British officers lost control of the rank and file, who murdered and pillaged. General Percy unlimbered his cannon; the balls tore down some walls but caused few casualties. In the taproom at Cooper's Tavern two drinking companions were shot when they resisted.

Two others, old men hiding in the cellar, were bayoneted. The soldiers broke into Thomas Russell's store (FIGURE 46), carried off what they could, and left the rum and molasses taps running all over the floor. Eighty-year-old veteran Samuel Whittemore fired his musket and two pistols at a British flanking party before they shot, bayoneted, and clubbed him, and left him for dead. But a spark of life lingered in his ancient frame; his wounds were dressed and, to everybody's amazement, he lived for another eighteen years! Nor did he ever regret what he had done.

Old Jason Russell elected to stay and defend his home, which he said was his castle. He died in his own doorway; his wife found his body with those of eleven other dead minutemen in the south room when she returned. The house still stands, and the bullet holes can yet be seen. The

Figure 46

twelve were buried in a common grave behind the church, where the old headstone records that Jason Russell was "barbarously murdered in his own house by Gage's bloody troops."

The day after the battle Hannah Winthrop, who with her ailing husband was a refugee from Charlestown, near Boston, went through the place and later wrote to a friend of "our passing through the bloody field of Menotomy, which was strewn with mangled bodies. We met one affectionate father with a cart looking for his murdered son and picking up his neighbors who had fallen in battle in order for their burial."[5]

All this the boy Samuel Wilson lived through and some of it he must have seen. Many of the women and children had gone up to the Prentiss house on the hill for safety, but it would have been hard to keep an active nine-year-old boy there in the presence of such great events, especially when the British wagons were lying on their sides in the hollow, with so many souvenirs to be acquired. It must have made a deep impression on his

young mind to have been present at the birth of American liberty.

In 1780, when Samuel was fourteen, his father decided to sell out and go to New Hampshire, where some friends had already preceded them. Accordingly he sold the Menotomy place to Thomas Russell, the storekeeper, and also disposed of a farm at Medford, taking his pay in Continental money. This was worth so little that he had to pay three thousand dollars of it for one yoke of oxen to help in the moving. The rest he used to buy a hundred-acre farm near the hamlet of Mason, New Hampshire, a few miles north of the Massachusetts line. There the family lived in a house (FIGURE 47) that is still standing, nearly as sound as the day it was built, the low ceilings, broad wall paneling, and wide floor boards testifying to its antiquity.

Young Sam Wilson trod those boards, and we can be sure that he ranged through the woods for game, keeping a wary eye open for the wildcats and bears which were still plentiful in those days. Nor is it hard to imagine the Wilson family

48

gathered about the fireplace of a winter's evening talking about Sam's two older brothers, Joseph and Edward, who had gone away to fight in General Washington's army. Sam himself saw no action.[6]

Luckily, both of the Wilson boys came home safely. Sam continued to live in Mason for another seven years after the end of the war. Mason Center is still the kind of a dreamy little place where a hound dog can slumber peacefully in the middle of the road. Dominating the village green is the square white house which in those days was the residence of the town's leading citizen, Captain Benjamin Mann, a veteran of Bunker Hill. Captain Mann's house was also the local store and tavern, as well as a place of resort for the countryside. To serve his guests the Captain had a free Negro named Christopher, whose wife did the cooking.

An occasional guest was the Captain's young nephew, John Chapman, from Lunenberg, Massachusetts. John was destined to write his own unique page in American history and folklore — as Johnny Appleseed.

Sam Wilson found a good many reasons to visit the Mann establishment, the most important one being the Captain's pretty daughter Betsey. It is not likely that they had gone to school together, since Sam was seven years older than the winsome Miss Mann. Certain it is, however, that their romance during the years after the war proved to both of them that they were meant for each other. It had to be that way to survive the long separation that followed, while Sam was out west seeking his fortune. He was obviously determined to make his way in the world before he took Betsey away from her comfortable lot as the daughter of Mason's most affluent citizen. Betsey prom-

Figure 47

ised to wait and, for eight mortal years, wait she did. That she had many an opportunity to forget her vow we can be sure, for she had ben favored with good looks and a joyous spirit as well as material blessings. We can only conclude that there must have been something special about the tall youth who waved good-by to her as he set out afoot over the ridges and through the forests of the storied Hudson Valley — something that set him apart from all the other young men who passed through her life. Was it his friendliness, his love of a good joke? He was known for that in later years. Or was it his bold imagination, his restless striving to better his lot and build large enterprises? For these, as time would show, he certainly possessed. His, too, was the sense of patriotism and responsibility which repeatedly during his long life was to inspire him to assume civic leadership in good causes.

One February day in 1789 Sam started west for a place called Vanderheyden, traveling afoot with his brother Ebenezer. It was nearly 150 miles from Mason to Vanderheyden, and it probably seemed farther still to the two Wilson boys. Breaking trail through the snow by day and huddling around a campfire by night, the trip must have taken them from ten days to two weeks.

The village of Vanderheyden had some natural advantages which attracted travelers and settlers. Well-positioned seven miles north of Albany on the east side of the Hudson, it was at the head of navigation and also at the point where the roads from the east converged. Farmers living south of the Mohawk River favored it as more convenient than New City (Lansingburgh), while those farther north, from the Lake Champlain area, soon discovered that they got higher prices for their produce there than in either of the other markets.

In January, 1789, the freeholders decided that the town needed a new name, shorter and easier to remember. Accordingly, they chose Troy, which was in keeping with the classical tradition that was spawning such upstate New York names as Rome, Utica, Syracuse, Ithaca, and Delphi. After some protests and not a little derision, everybody began to use the new name except the Patroon, Jacob D. Van der Heyden, who steadfastly continued to inscribe his own name on documents throughout the years.

The Wilson brothers arrived the month after Vanderheyden got its new name. They were young and vigorous — Samuel twenty-two and Ebenezer twenty-seven — both eager to make friends and get on. They began brickmaking the summer following their arrival, using clay from a bank on the west slope of Mount Ida, just above what is now the Ferry Street end of the Sixth Avenue tunnel. Previously most of the brick used locally had been imported from Holland as ballast in sailing ships, which came up the Hudson as far as Albany.[7]

The first building to use this brick was built by James Spencer in 1792 at the northwest corner of Second and Albany (Broadway) streets, on Washington Square triangle. The Wilsons also furnished brick for the first courthouse and jail, erected in 1793. Troy and Lansingburgh engaged in keen competition for this honor. The

50

Figure 49

decision as to location was to be made on the basis of which town subscribed the most to the building fund. Colonel Albert Pawling, county sheriff and a resident of Troy, took subscriptions as he traveled through Rensselaer County on official business. Samuel Wilson pledged four pounds, and Ebenezer three (FIGURE 48). With one thousand pounds subscribed, Troy won out. The courthouse was built at the southeast corner of Congress and

Figure 48 (below)

Second streets, with the jail just behind it. Shown here (FIGURE 49) behind the Presbyterian meetinghouse in the foreground are (left to right) the jail, courthouse, and Moulton's Coffeehouse.

Until the completion of the jail, a room in the courthouse with barred door and grated windows served as a place of confinement. In the courtyard were a pillory and a whipping post. Debtors were immured in the jail, and frequently inserted piteous appeals for aid in the local press, of which the following is an example:

TO THE HUMANE AND BENEVOLENT — It is through real necessity that the debtors in jail make known their situation to the public. With diffidence they solicit the citizens

51

to help them so far as to keep them from hunger; as the law gives no relief, and consequently, if unable to help themselves and unassisted by a charitable community, they must inevitably starve. One of their number is two hundred miles from his friends and family, without money for credit.

Samuel and Ebenezer had entered the meat-packing business in 1793. It was in connection with this venture that Sam was, all unwittingly, to win enduring fame. Their establishment was on a "creek in a meadow not far from where the Poestenkill enters the Hudson."[8] This site is between the present Adams and Jefferson streets, a little east of River Street. The meat was salted and transformed into the "canned willie" so well known to generations of troopers, after which it was packed in quarters at a yard on the south side of Ferry Street between First and Second streets.

About that time Samuel and his brother constructed a dock at the foot of Ferry Street, where they loaded their barrels of beef and pork onto their own sloops, which then took the cargoes down the Hudson. And in order to integrate their packing business, they built a farmhouse near what is now the junction of Cottage and Fifteenth streets. In the fields were pastured and fattened for market the large herds of cattle and swine which were required to assure a steady supply for the packing yard. The site of this farm was directly north of the present Liberty and Division streets, which end at Mount Ida. The property became known as Wilson's Bowl, or Wilson's Hollow, because of the conformation of the land there, and the forested area along the ridge was known as Wilson's Woods. The greater part of the Wilson holdings is now included within Prospect Park.

The town was still quite rural in 1793, with many trees and bushes in evidence and the stores and warehouses going up mostly on the west side of River Street. On March 8 of that year, for an annual ground rent of thirty shillings, Jacob D. Van der Heyden leased to Samuel Wilson the west half of the lot on the northwest corner of Second and Ferry streets, where Samuel proceeded to erect a small frame dwelling, and there he lived for many years (FIGURE 50).

Troy continued to grow. By 1794 the population had reached nearly five hundred. There was a smallpox epidemic that year, and the preventive measures taken led to a counting of the citizenry. Travelers from New England bound for the western country often liked what they saw at the ferry crossing and decided to stay. From lofts along the river, spouts poured grain into the holds of fat schooners and sloops. Ox-wains and horse-drawn wagons lumbered in from the country laden with the products of the Dutch dairies and farms. The clang of the blacksmith's anvil was heard, the sharp crack of the stage driver's whip and the shouts of the rivermen. A traveler in 1795 reported that

. . . the houses are very neat and numerous; almost every house contains a shop; the inns are excellent; vessels are moored near all the keys; tan-yards, potash works, rope walks and mills are either in full work or building. . . . A Mr. Taylor, who possesses about one hundred acres near Poestenkill Creek, has erected there two grist mills, two saw mills, and one paper mill.[9]

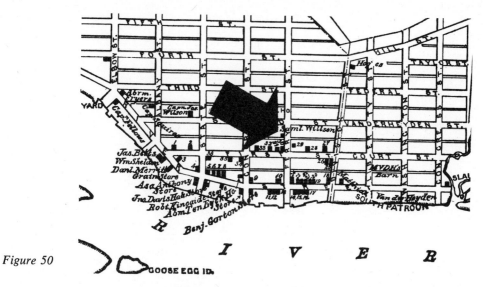

Figure 50

Troy was swept by a wave of enthusiasm for projects designed to connect the waters of Lake Champlain and those of the western lakes with the Hudson by means of canals, locks, and dams. Cheap, easy transportation was all-important, and companies were formed to push all kinds of schemes, including lotteries. But the aims of these were not to be realized for another generation.

Though Sam had devoted much time and effort to business, he had not forgotten Betsey back in New Hampshire. In 1797 he returned to Mason, where he and Betsey were married on January 3 by the Reverend Ebenezer Hill, a long-time friend.[10] Sam was in his thirty-first year, Betsey her twenty-fourth. They rode back to Troy in a sleigh through the bright cold of the New England winter, bells tinkling merrily and Betsey's "settin'-out" dowry packed snugly on behind.

Samuel and Betsey had four children. The first, Polly, died in 1805 during her eighth year. Seven-year-old Sam fell from a wagon while "catching a ride" and died of a fractured skull in 1807. Another son, Benjamin, became an attorney and practiced in New York City. He died in 1859 of "Isthmus fever," having contracted the disease on a trip to California by way of Panama. He is buried in Troy's Oakwood Cemetery near his father and mother. Albert Wilson, born about 1805, was closest to his parents. He became a silversmith and banjo maker, living until 1866. With him the Wilsons passed their last days.[11]

The extent of Samuel's success may be judged from the fact that the Wilson and Mann families migrated almost en masse to Troy. Probably they were attracted by the same opportunities that converted Troy into a boom town during and immediately after the War of 1812 (FIGURE 51). Certainly the firm of E. & S. Wilson enjoyed a period of real prosperity while they were busily engaged in filling their war contracts, and we may suppose that Uncle Sam found places for a good many of his relatives in the large work force

Figure 51

which he employed. A few years later he went into partnership with one of them, probably James Mann, his brother-in-law, selling groceries and dry goods as Wilson & Mann. This association lasted only a short time, however. Evidence has been produced that Uncle Sam also took a flyer in the distillery business. Meanwhile the brickyard continued to operate. As late as 1833 Samuel Wilson was making public acknowledgment of help from his friends and fellow citizens "who have subscribed so liberally to make up his loss at his bricking establishment during the recent freshet."

After the war Uncle Sam and his younger brother, Uncle Nat, set up another meat-packing operation in Catskill, New York, where they lived for some time in the Haxtun house. They brought with

them from Troy some of their best hands, including a fabulous character named Jonas W. Gleason who was a "boss butcher." Gleason had lungs like a smith's bellows. He was an ambitious man, and something of an orator. He made Fourth of July addresses which were punctuated by discharges from the "mouse-hole" of an anvil. At the "blow-outs" which signalized the close of the packing season, Jonas always led a procession of workers to the festive board, riding horseback, and wearing a huge pair of bullock livers as epaulets. Jonas was also foreman of the local hook and ladder company, addressing the members every month from the top of the ladder. And finally, he was the town auctioneer, a post for which his voice eminently qualified him.

An atmosphere of jocularity seems to

have pervaded Samuel Wilson's operations wherever he went. Part of this can be traced to Uncle Sam himself, who according to the testimony of his relatives and friends, would go to considerable length to make a good joke. For the rest, we can impute some of it to Jonas Gleason, whose talent for raillery made him the principal jester. As a boss of the yard, and the best-known character there aside from Uncle Sam himself, he would have been the man to welcome visitors. Therefore it is probable that Gleason was the Irishman referred to by Lucius Wilson, who made the observation that launched the Uncle Sam legend. And such are the ways of jokesters, that having made it, he doubtless kept on repeating it to all who would listen.

When did this happen? Lucius Wilson says that it was at a time when a large consignment was awaiting shipment. Since these barrels all bore the initials of the contractor, and deliveries on the contract were scheduled for the months of January through April, 1813, it would appear that the incident can be dated somewhere near the beginning of the delivery period, probably the first month. This would have given the story a few weeks to spread before the publication of the broadside with the earliest printed mention of Uncle Sam that spring.

Originally located in West Catskill near Hop-o'-Nose, the Wilson enterprise did so well that it was moved to "the Point," where it was much enlarged. Uncle Sam returned to Troy, leaving his brother to carry on.

A Catskill chronicler recalls that Uncle Sam's son Albert "was once most cruelly maltreated, by a teacher named Nutting, who, in his rage, pulled the hair from the boy's head, and otherwise mutilated him, and I well remember that there was a strong expression of indignation by the whole community at this act of brutality." He adds that Nutting was afterwards, and perhaps appropriately, selected as the principal of a female seminary! He continues:

The last time I saw the two brothers, Samuel and Nathaniel Wilson together, was in the summer of 1846, at the house of the elder, in Troy, where Nathaniel was on a visit. Time had then been pecking at them for about four-score years, but aside from a weakening of the knees, which Uncle Nat assured us was "a family complaint," the old mower had made but little impression on either of them. They cracked their jokes, and enjoyed their reminiscences of old times with all the zest of boyhood, and their hearty laughter rang out until Mount Ida sent its echoes to join in the hilarity.[12]

Uncle Nat remained in Catskill, and there he died in 1854, just nineteen days after Uncle Sam. He had four sons, of whom one, Francis, became president of the Catskill Bank.

It is recounted that on one occasion Uncle Sam found it necessary to go to Catskill on business. He embarked during a period of high water on a sloop commanded by Captain Abram Nash, a Troy carpenter. The latter was not well acquainted with the river, and ran the sloop into a cornfield. There it stayed until morning, when it was finally gotten off, and three days later it arrived at Catskill.

As the fame of Uncle Sam spread, the people of Catskill affixed a bronze tablet to a bridge near West Main Street where he and Uncle Nat lived, but this later disappeared.

After the birth of the Uncle Sam legend, Samuel Wilson was in constant demand as chairman of meetings, officer of clubs and civic groups, and member of committees for the reception of distinguished guests. Add to this his political activities on behalf of the Jacksonians, and it is evident that Uncle Sam led a busy life as one of Troy's best-known citizens. During the war he was the kind of man people thought of to serve on a committee to aid the families of soldiers away in the army. Later, he became a popular toastmaster, proposing this toast at a meeting of the Democratic Party: "The young men of Rensselaer! Animated by a glorious spirit of liberty, they have nobly manifested their desire of promoting the extension of Republican principles." And at another Jackson meeting called to celebrate the anniversary of the battle of New Orleans, he offered this one: "Hickory to lash the enemies of our country!" His devotion to Jackson caused him to be chosen one of a committee to receive the President on his tour of New England in 1833. Unhappily, the old warrior became ill en route. He managed to endure a round of public functions in Massachusetts, only to collapse in Concord, New Hampshire. Thus Troy never saw him, though it did play host that year to Henry Clay.

In 1824, Rufus Belknap published his journal of a trip to Troy from New York. He knew about the Uncle Sam story and reported that there was a blacksmith shop in Albany bearing the sign *Uncle Joe's Stables and Blacksmith Shop*. Belknap

asked the blacksmith if he was related to Uncle Sam. "His own brother," was the reply. This would have been Uncle Sam's elder brother Joseph, who evidently followed Samuel to the Hudson Valley.

The story crediting Samuel Wilson as the source of the term "Uncle Sam" appeared repeatedly in the newspapers of both Troy and New York City, and there is no indication that it was ever doubted or denied. After one such notice the Troy editor ran the following comment: "It is proper for us to remark that the individuals (Messrs. Ebenezer and Samuel Wilson) are now alive and residents of this city."[13] Despite this, there is no evidence that Uncle Sam ever took very seriously his privileged status as the patron saint of the republic.

Aunt Betsey Wilson was a fitting spouse for Uncle Sam. Both delighted in having young people around them, and social affairs for that purpose were of frequent occurrence. Betsey Wilson has been described as a woman of great charm and dignity. She was one of the six managers of the Ladies' Benevolent Society, established in 1830 to render assistance to indigent women and children.[14]

In 1837 Uncle Sam was chairman of the Democratic Committee. By this time he was seventy-one and becoming less active. He came of a long-lived family; his mother; several of his brothers were octogenarians.

There are few references to him during the next fifteen years. The country was busy with the Mexican War and the antislavery troubles. Uncle Sam and the War of 1812 were back numbers. Samuel Wilson lived peaceably in his house at 144

Ferry Street, the third one he had built in Troy, which is still standing and should be restored as a national shrine (FIGURE 52). It was here that Lucius Wilson remembers him as rocking on a side porch through the long summer evenings — a porch which has long since disappeared.

Uncle Sam had been failing physically over a period of years. However, as late as 1848 he had paid two thousand dollars for a lot, which indicates that he was still able to transact business. During the last year before his death he was confined to his home. He passed away there July 31, 1854. The local papers chronicling his death also carried stories of the worst cholera epidemic in history. Up to thirty deaths were reported in the Troy-Greenbush area alone. And to make it worse, the weather was unusually hot even for July. The Troy *Northern Budget* marked the event with an editorial in which it observed that Samuel Wilson

Figure 52

. . . was himself engaged in, and prosecuted successfully, at least four distinct kinds of business, employing about 200 hands constantly, while he took the oversight of each particular branch, in connection with his brother Eben. He prosecuted the mercantile business in connection with slooping, the brick-making business very extensively; the distillery business; farming, on a pretty large scale, and the slaughtering business on an extensive plan. During the War of 1812 he supplied the army very generally, especially at the north, from his very extensive yards. His tact for managing laborers was very peculiar; he would always say "come boys" instead of "go," and thereby secured a greater amount of labor than ordinary men. His success in business he mainly attributed to a strict *system* in his plans, and the constant habit of early rising, and to this habit he undoubtedly owed his uniform good health, and his useful life. He had eight brothers and two sisters, all of whom were tenacious of this habit, and all but two are now dead, but their ages averaged a full 80 years each. In his political creed he was strictly Republican and was warmly attached to the Democratic party, and in the election of General Jackson to the Presidency he took a very active part, serving as a *standing chairman* of the party both at his first and second election. In his religious creed he was tolerant to all. He was united to no church, but at the age of three score years his mind became deeply imbued with religion, and feeling his responsibility to his Maker, he solemnly dedicated himself to God and united with the Presbyterian Church in this city.[15] His walk and conversation since this solemn transition, evidenced the sincerity of his profession, and he has left a pleasing assurance both to the church and his friends that he now "Rests from his labors and his works follow him."

Oddly enough, the accounts of his death in the Troy papers made no reference to the Uncle Sam legend. However, the Albany *Evening Journal* carried the following story on August 1:

"UNCLE SAM" — The death of Samuel Wilson, an aged, worthy and formerly enterprising citizen of Troy, will remind those who were familiar with the incidents of the War of 1812, of the origin of the popular sobriquet for the "United States." Mr. Wilson was an extensive packer, had the contract for supplying the northern army with beef and pork. He was everywhere known and spoken of as "Uncle Sam," and the "U. S." branded on the heads of barrels for the army were at first taken to be the initials of "Uncle Sam" Wilson, but finally lost their local significance and became, throughout the army, the familiar term for "United States." . . .

The same story appeared a few days later in both the New York *Tribune* and the New York *Post*.

Samuel Wilson was buried the day after he died in Mount Ida Cemetery. Later the body was removed to Oakwood Cemetery, where now rests all that was mortal of Uncle Sam, together with his wife Betsey, who survived until 1863, his son Benjamin and the two children, Polly and Samuel, who died in infancy. Albert's grave is in Mount Ida Cemetery. Captain Benjamin Mann, Betsey Wilson's father, was buried in the old Troy Cemetery near Cypress Street, as was Uncle Sam's father, Edward Wilson, who died in 1816 at the age of eighty-two. This cemetery was so long neglected that even the locations were lost. Uncle Sam's mother, Lucy Francis Wilson,[16] returned to Mason and died there in 1835, aged ninety-six years.

Figure 53

Uncle Sam's plot in Oakwood is well marked and cared for, and is frequently the scene of patriotic ceremonies. In 1931, Marion Wilson Sheldon, a granddaughter, dedicated a four-ton granite monument to his memory at the grave site (FIGURE 53).

Few tourists visit the grave, principally because the Uncle Sam story has never been widely told outside of Troy. Various efforts have been made by Troy organizations to raise a large permanent memorial to Samuel Wilson, presumably somewhere in the area where he lived and worked. As more Americans learn about him, it is probable that in the years to come these plans will be realized.

7: The Legend Grows

There may be some deeper significance in the choice of *Uncle* Sam rather than a father or mother symbol as in many other countries: for example, Mother India, and the Little Father of all the Russias. Having had difficulties with the system under which a monarch represented the benevolent father, Americans were not too anxious to acquire another such powerful parent. Indeed, the central idea of the new Government was a distrust of too much power and the use of checks and balances to prevent its misuse by any man or group. Hence, perhaps, the immediate popularity of the Uncle Sam symbol. An uncle is usually a remote but beneficent stem off the parental branch who brings goodies to American children, tells them stories, and generally makes himself popular without using the rod of authority reserved for parents. In many families it is usual for close adult friends to be endowed by children with the honorary title of "Uncle" or "Aunt." It may be indicative of the American attitude toward government that the symbol for it is an uncle, and as such, an oblique rather than a direct connection. This perfectly positions government in the U. S. as a necessary operation which must never under any circumstances forget that it is *not* a father and has no right to act like one. In fact, before any American is taken to the woodshed with a razor strop, figuratively speaking, he must be given a bill of particulars and the right to have counsel.

Uncle Sam remains frozen in the garb of the early 1800's. Yet his spirit goes marching on in hundreds of different interpretations. For a cartoonist, doing Uncle Sam is a little like an actor's playing Hamlet. They all take a crack at it sooner or later, but few do it really well. And fewer still leave any lingering and permanent impressions on the role which are historic and good enough to last.

Uncle remains the shrewd old party who is Brother Jonathan given official status. He is the antique farmer out of a Dion Boucicault melodrama. He is the Yankee who trudged across the land peddling needles and notions, and in so doing, gave his name and many of his personal characteristics to the nation. He may seem to be the "Wal, I swan" type, gawking at the big town with his toil-worn hands clasped under his coattails to protect his cowhide wallet from the city sharpers. Yet everybody knows that he is really smart as all get-out, even though he may buy a Brooklyn Bridge now and then.

The cartoonists' favorite pose for him seems to be as in desperate straits — bilked, puzzled, disgusted, riled, at his wits' end. Seldom is he shown happy and at peace with himself and the world, which again may be only a reflection of the times we live in. There seems to be almost a rule about this. Uncle is usually on the short end. He is definitely the fall guy, and as such, the visible embodiment of problems and protests. He is squarely in the center of the yeasty ferment of the democratic process at work — the opposition of opinions and forces that creates our national policies.

There is no evidence that any of the cartoonists who have kept Uncle Sam in the public eye through the years ever saw the original Uncle Sam. The earliest versions were widely different and did not

Figure 54

begin to assume the present form until the period of the Civil War. A number of local characters have been put forward as the models of the present cartoon version, including George Buchanan, who lived in Woburn, Massachusetts, and died in 1917, and Colonel Ellsworth Phelps, a Civil War veteran born in 1826, who was well known in Washington and was celebrated by the newspapers for his resemblance to the cartoon figure.

In 1908 a student of Americana named

Figure 55

Albert Matthews undertook to track down the sources of the Uncle Sam story. He located its origin in the War of 1812 period rightly enough, but could find no drawings prior to 1852. He did not discover that the eyewitness account had been so widely reprinted in 1830, and apparently he did not know of Lucius Wilson and his testimony, which was not written down until 1917. Nor did he know of William Henry Jackson's story. Matthews was skeptical, one of his principal reasons being that it had taken so long for the cartoonists to put Uncle Sam on paper. And for years the 1852 cartoon by Frank H. T. Bellew was accepted as the first (FIGURE 54).

But it was not. The first drawing of Uncle Sam discovered so far appeared twenty years earlier. He made his graphic debut in an unsigned lithograph issued in 1832 and entitled "Uncle Sam in Danger" (FIGURE 55). It is not much technically, but it conveys the bitterness over Andrew Jackson's efforts to destroy the Bank of the United States, in which he was ultimately to succeed. Like most cartoons of the period, this is an attack on Jackson. He has just opened a vein in the right arm of a seated Uncle Sam, who is smooth-shaven, rather young, and attired in a striped robe. The blood is being caught in a pan, labeled "Safety Fund," by Amos Kendall, Secretary of the Treas-

61

Figure 56

ury, to whom Jackson is directing the quaintly spelled command: "Hold the Bason, Amos, this is merely an Experament, but I take the Responsibility." In the foreground Van Buren listens to Uncle Sam's plaintive query as to the pills which have been prescribed — "Do you recommend them, Dr?" — and replies, "I cannot commit myself for these pills are too purging." Behind Jackson the uniformed figure of Major Jack Downing declares dolefully, " 'Twixt the Ginril (since he's ta'en to Doctring) and the little Dutch Potercary Uncle Sam stands no more chance than a stump tail'd Bull in fly time." Another character, probably Senator Thomas Benton, defends the pills.

The next version elaborates the same theme, but there are interesting variations (FIGURE 56). Uncle Sam is older, and his robe is definitely the American flag. Jackson and Benton, in old-fashioned costumes, propose respectively diet and "juice of humbug," while Van Buren, as Aunt Matty, is warned by Uncle Sam that "if you don't leave off ruining my *Constitution* with your quack nostrums, I'll soon give you your walking ticket . . . and call in Doctor Biddle to prescribe for me." Outside, Biddle is seen arriving and is being greeted by Brother Jonathan. This is one of the very few instances where Uncle Sam and Brother Jonathan appear in the same cartoon, and reinforces the

62

Figure 57

assumption that Uncle Sam represents the Government, while Brother Jonathan stands for the people. Behind Uncle Sam the American eagle is threatening to fly away, since starvation awaits here. The list of failures which Uncle Sam holds, and which seems to be the cause of his malady, dates this piece as just after the panic of 1837, probably the next year.

Frequently during this period the figure of Major Jack Downing appears in the cartoons as an aide to Jackson. He was strictly imaginary, being the creation of Seba Smith of the Portland, Maine, *Courier,* yet the letters supposedly written by him were the best-read newspaper feature of the day. The Major was represented as the confidant of the President, and as such accompanied him on all his journeys. Jackson appreciated the Major Downing letters as much as anybody, and once said that he was probably Van Buren in disguise. Downing, like Brother Jonathan, and the real-life Finley Peter Dunne and Will Rogers much later, was the voice of the American people. For a while it almost seemed that he might replace Brother Jonathan and Uncle Sam. But he was too closely tied to Jackson, and when that doughty old warrior passed from the scene, Major Downing soon disappeared, too.

One of the very few cartoons favorable to Jackson was drawn by E. W. Clay and published by H. R. Robinson in 1833 (FIGURE 57). It was "The Downfall of Mother Bank, Draw'd off from Natur by Zek Downing, Neffu to Major Jack Down-

63

Figure 58

ing." Jackson holds his order for the removal of public funds from the Bank of the United States, which is shown collapsing while its president, Nicholas Biddle, who is depicted as a fiend, flees with his retainers.

One of the earliest representations of the Democratic donkey appears in "Race over Uncle Sam's Course — 4th March, 1833," published about 1832 and ascribed to D. C. Johnston (FIGURE 58). Andrew Jackson's lowly steed, with Van Buren as a monkey riding behind, stumbles on a rock labeled "Bank U. S." as Henry Clay, on a horse, forges ahead.

Hardly better drawn than a comic valentine is "Uncle Sam's Pet Pups," published by Elton in 1840 (FIGURE 59). The anonymous artist shows Uncle Sam urging two canines with the heads of Jackson

and Van Buren toward a hard-cider barrel into which Mother Bank is crawling. The figure astride the barrel is probably General William Henry Harrison.

Cartoons had not yet reached the public press except in a few isolated instances. They were mainly published as broadsides for hand-to-hand circulation or posting. Used this way in an era when people had fewer claims on their attention, these pictorial jibes were widely seen, and the points they made were understood even by those who did not read newspapers or attend political meetings. Sometimes portfolios of cartoons were rented out to serve as conversation pieces at social gatherings. One of the best-known publishers was H. R. Robinson, from whose shop at 52 Courtlandt Street, New York City, there issued a stream of caricatures satirizing

64

Figure 59

the events of Jackson's and Van Buren's administrations. Robinson bought the works of the best cartoonists of the day, in addition to which he designed many others himself, drawing directly on stone. Robinson also produced maps and plans, but cartoons seem to have been his first love.

There were several reasons for the new interest in caricature which became evident in the thirties. One was the increasing use of lithography, which provided a simpler and cheaper method of reproduction. Instead of cutting the picture in wood or metal, the artist worked on a flat stone, from which the picture was printed. Lithography favored more delicate halftone effects than the older processes. It was faster, too; the artist alert to current events could capture the essence of a new crisis as soon as it occurred and see his cartoons offered for sale on the streets in a few hours.

For example, the northern boundary of Maine had been in dispute between the United States and Great Britain ever since the Revolution. In the thirties this nearly provoked armed conflict. Of special interest in this connection is the 1832 cartoon (FIGURE 60) "A general arguing of the Maine Question, or John Bull's Bully trying to frighten Jonathan out of Title and Timber." Wellington, as Prime Minister, asserts British rights to timberland in northern Maine. Jonathan is undaunted; holding a codfish in one hand, he points at the Duke with the other as he says, "I'll bet you a four pence, you Sarpent! UNCLE SAM will make you pay for every splinter on't. He can lick the whole grist of your Generals in no time. . . ." This establishes Jonathan as Uncle Sam's nephew. James Akin, who drew it, was one of the leading cartoonists of the day.

Equally responsible for the new popularity of the cartoon were the waves of

65

Figure 60

passion — pro and con — that rolled through the Jackson era. Whether one liked Old Hickory or just as emphatically disliked him, he was not a man to be ignored. The frontiersman, who hadn't had too much truck with other administrations, and rather distrusted government anyway, held strong views about the victor of New Orleans, and they were likely to be favorable. Even so, most of the cartoons were derisive or sarcastic, probably because they were printed in the northern cities populated largely by his political opponents.

Uncle Sam figures prominently in these cartoons. He has not yet been cast in a single mold; each artist depicts his own version. Edward Clay and William Williams dress him in street clothes. D. C. Johnston, Frank Bellew, and others maintain the Brother Jonathan identification, evidently preferring to stay with a familiar symbol rather than to venture with one which up to that time had been mainly verbal.

Quite different is "Uncle Sam and his Servants," by H. Bucholzer, published by J. Baillie in 1844 (FIGURE 61). Here Uncle Sam is an elderly man in knee breeches and a broad-brimmed flat hat. He is aiming a kick at John Tyler, who tries to bar Clay, Calhoun, Polk, and

Figure 61

Jackson from entering Uncle Sam's house.

Four years later, another version of this colonial Uncle Sam was produced by T. Horton to promote the presidential aspirations of General Zachary Taylor. Taylor, who already has the lease, watches the discomfiture of his rival, Lewis Cass, with a satisfied smirk (FIGURE 62). There follows a song in ten verses entitled "Old Zack Taylor is the Man," to be sung to the tune of "Yankee Doodle."

The changing aspect of both Uncle Sam and Jonathan, resulting in the submergence of the latter, was expedited by the strength of Jackson's personal leadership. This was demonstrated by Jackson's victory in the clash with Vice President John Calhoun on the issue of states' rights, when the President threatened to hang the great nullifier "as high as Haman." Jackson also contributed to the growth of Federal power by his successful fight on the Bank of the United States. When this national institution came up for renewal of its charter, he declared war on it because he alleged it mixed too much politics with business. And toward the end of his administration, Jackson

67

UNCLE SAM.—You look very pretty, Mr. Gass, but you can't come in; I've had so many of your sort already that I hardly know my own farm.

Figure 62

gave national pride a lift by collecting damages from France for property damage done by Napoleon, though he had to put the Navy on a war footing to do it.

In these times Jackson might be called a tyrant and a warmonger. He was called worse names in his own. But like Theodore Roosevelt, another President who sustained Federal authority and made the cartoonists happy, he centralized interest in Uncle Sam and all his doings. Not for another generation would there be in the White House a President who would afford as likely a subject, and who would do as much, amid the confusion of civil conflict, to reassert Uncle Sam's status as the symbol of the Union.

Meanwhile, the nation suffered through the lean times of 1837 to 1841, and as always after such a financial storm, went on to greater expansion and more prosperity than had been thought possible. Longer and longer grew the lines of prairie schooners heading west. Expansion brought conflict with Mexico; President Polk offered to buy California for twenty-five million dollars and New Mexico for another five million dollars. When these overtures failed, war was only a matter of time and was finally precipitated by a series of bloody clashes along the disputed Texas-Mexico border. After it was over the United States had won what is now the Southwest, and eventually by the terms of the treaty and the subsequent Gadsden Purchase, paid nearly as much for it as we had offered in the first place.

Done with the spirit that distinguished all the cartoons of E. W. Clay is "Uncle Sam's Taylorifics," dated 1846 (FIGURE 63). In rather complicated action of which each element is labeled, Uncle Sam uses

Figure 63

both his boot and a big pair of scissors on the Mexican. Meanwhile John Bull fishes for more of Oregon. This is typical of the etchings, engravings and lithographs in which Clay produced so many significant social and political caricatures.

8: Rumblings of Civil War

During the years preceding the Civil War, one of the most powerful influences in shaping the character representing the United States was the London *Punch*. In particular the cartoons of John Leech and John Tenniel gave visual expression to British opinions concerning the actions of Brother Jonathan. *Punch* called him that long after the name had been abandoned elsewhere — did not transfer to Uncle Sam, in fact, until the turn of the century. The reason for this preference is probably that Jonathan was a Yankee folk figure to whom it was easy to feel superior. This was especially true because many Britishers liked to think of the name "Jonathan" as derived from that of John Bull himself, of whom Jonathan was the unregenerate offspring — a junior and a jackanapes, untutored in the civilized manners of his long-suffering parent.

The name "Uncle Sam," on the other hand, carried with it a great deal more dignity and significance. Using it would have been, in effect, recognizing that the United States had acquired senior status — was itself a nation to be deferred to and reckoned with. This would not have accorded with the popular British view of America during much of the nineteenth century. Further, the British had a sort of sympathetic attachment for Jonathan because of their blood ties with him. They relished many of his misadventures and felt a certain pride in his achievements. Jonathan with his English language and laws was still a chip off the old block, and though he had fallen into many prodigal ways, he had good qualities which could be attributed to his ancestry.

But to the British Uncle Sam was a wholly alien concept, charged with overtones of rebellion and independence; he stood for the complete and successful defiance of authority in the name of freedom from the paternal guiding strings.[1] Moreover, it was the queer ideas represented by Uncle Sam which had led Jonathan astray in the first place, and which encouraged him in his recalcitrant behavior.

Many American cartoonists also favored Jonathan over Uncle Sam in the years before 1860. In general, those who worked in lighter vein usually chose Jonathan, while more serious efforts involving the Government itself featured Uncle Sam. Physically, Jonathan was usually depicted as younger and more callow, though as time went on he grew to look more and more like Uncle Sam, who was never shown as other than a mature man. With the Civil War and the final assertion of the power of the central Government, Jonathan went into eclipse in America, and in a few more years had merged entirely with the victorious symbol of the Federal Union.

It is interesting that the Jonathan depicted by the artists of *Punch* developed some of the modern characteristics of Uncle Sam earlier than American artists did. This may be attributed in part to the superb draftsmanship of the cartoons by Leech and Tenniel and their fertility of resource in catching the Yankee habits and mannerisms.

Through the years *Punch* reflects with considerable fidelity the ups and downs of British-American relations, which had a way (not unlike today) of running into a crisis every few years. Jonathan was shown sometimes as a precocious but ill-

Figure 64

mannered moppet being censured by John Bull or Grandmother Britannia. In other cartoons he appears as the callous and saturnine slavemaster whose principal concerns are money and brawling, and whose idea of polite conversation is "Let's liquor up!"

In a Leech cartoon of 1846, "Young Yankee Noodle Teaching Grandmother Britannia to Suck Eggs," Jonathan holds an egg labeled "Oregon" as the old lady regards him almost with affection (FIGURE 64). It was the time of the border controversy that had brought forth the slogan of the American settlers "Fifty-four forty or fight!"

Typical of the other view is the wry commentary of *Punch* cartoonist Dickie Doyle, published in 1847 (FIGURE 65),

71

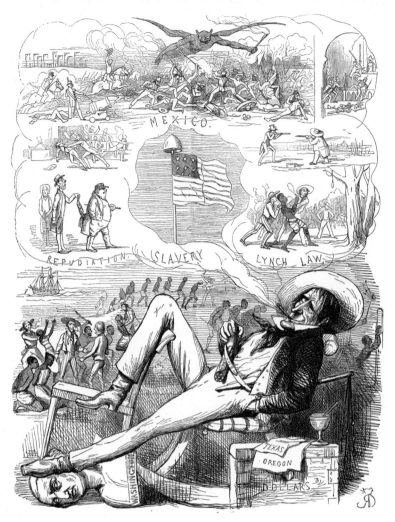

Figure 65

entitled "The Land of Liberty — Recommended to the Consideration of Brother Jonathan." This is an excellent evocation of the then current British stereotype of America. Jonathan, a lean "segar"-smoking hellion with a pepperbox revolver stuck in his belt and a drink alongside, sprawls on his money chest with one foot on a bust of Washington. Shown behind him are the horrors of the slave trade and the slaughter of the Mexican War.

"Texas" and "Oregon" appear on documents at his elbow.

Another Leech cartoon of 1848 (FIGURE 66), "Liberty, Equality, Fraternity," is "Dedicated to the Smartest Nation in All Creation." It shows Jonathan, with his inseparable cheroot, julep, and shotgun, watching Liberty, who has a false face, flogging a Negro. He observes, "Oh, ain't we a deal better than other people! I guess we're a most splendid example to

72

Figure 66

Figure 67

them thunderin' old Monarchies!" Having liberated the slaves in her own West Indian colonies as early as 1833, Britain took exception to the oft-proclaimed American devotion to the ideals of liberty. It is interesting that this image of Jonathan as a hard-bitten slaveholder drew largely from the American South. Yet *Punch* found it quite easy in later years to shift emphasis from the enormities of the slave power to the misdeeds of the Lincoln Administration, which it belabored without stint or limit.

Another storm blew up between the two countries in the late fifties over the question of the Canadian fishing fleets. Britain even sent armed vessels to keep New England fishermen out of waters claimed by the Canadians as their ex-

clusive preserve. The usual threats were exchanged, but all was settled amicably by a treaty recognizing the rights of both parties. *Punch* highlighted this situation in an 1856 cartoon (FIGURE 67), "Please Return a Favourable Answer," apparently by Leech, which shows John Bull, wearing sword and pistols and backed by his men-o'-war, extending the hand of fellowship to Jonathan as he says, "Come, Jonathan, why should we fight — Am I not a man, and a brother?" The ironic twist here is that the latter part of the query had been the slogan of the anti-slavery movement ever since its founding at the end of the eighteenth century. And as Jonathan contemplates, a cat-o'-nine-tails protrudes from his pocket. Leech made this slave whip one of Jonathan's

Figure 68

Figure 69 (below)

trademarks for years. Another Leechism are the pantaloons, on which the stars are at the bottom with stripes above. This never caught on to any extent with other artists. Stars appeared at various times on the coat, the lapels only, the hat, and the waistcoat, and still do. But most cartoonists have now settled on striped trousers and hat, with a hatband of stars.[2]

The American cartoonists Thomas Nast and Joseph Keppler have long been credited with giving Uncle Sam his whiskers, just after the Civil War. Actually, Leech drew a Jonathan with chin whiskers for *Punch* as early as 1856 (FIGURE 68). This cartoon is captioned "The Spoilt Child." John Bull, conscious of America's

74

Figure 70

internal difficulties, observes with an air of paternal forbearance, "I don't like to correct him just now, because he's about his teeth, and sickening for the measles — but he certainly deserves a clout on the head."

Later in the year *Punch* ran a poem on "The Split in the States," the final stanza of which asserted:

> Strange may it seem, and yet is not;
> The peril of the Free
> All springs from one unhappy blot,
> The Taint of Slavery.
> That, that is all you have to dread:
> Get rid of that and go a-head!

Ever alert to lecture Jonathan on his shortcomings, John Bull took him to task again a year later, which was President Buchanan's first in the White House. A period of expansion and extravagance had resulted in the depression of 1857. Father Bull says, "The fact is, Jonathan, both you and your wife have been living too

75

Figure 71

fast." In this drawing (FIGURE 69) Leech reverses the design of the pantaloons, stars above the stripes below. The beard remains.

French artists of the time also took occasional digs at American foibles. They followed the lead of the British in preferring Jonathan to Uncle Sam. One such cartoon of the Civil War period, drawn by Jules Pelcoq for *Actualités* (FIGURE 70), shows Jonathan reviewing his "irregular troops" as he prepares to leave for war. Jonathan is bearded and his head looks like an unkempt haystack. He wears a striped cravat. His "troops" consist of a Bloomer Girl, a Quaker, and Uncle Tom. This reflects the opinion, widely held in Europe, that the people of the North would not fight to stop secession, and could not prevent it even if they tried.

While these new and unflattering versions of Jonathan were finding expression on the other side of the Atlantic, American cartoonists, with few exceptions, stayed with the more usual design. In 1858 *Harper's Weekly* ran a drawing (FIGURE 71) of "Mr. Jonathan Rarey, the Great Bull-Tamer, as he appeared before the World in his highly successful feat of

Figure 72

Taming the English Bull." John S. Rarey was a noted horse-tamer of the day. Another (FIGURE 72) from the same periodical two years later celebrates the arrival of the Japanese delegation in the United States, returning the visit of Commodore Matthew Perry's squadron to Japan in 1853. A rather smug and self-satisfied Jonathan says "Ah! Mister, and, pray, what can I do for you?"

But in that crucial year of 1860 Americans were mainly concerned with the threat of civil war. As the Democratic Convention met at Charleston, and feuding delegates from North and South decided to go their separate ways, *Frank Leslie's Illustrated Newspaper* cartooned their thrusts at the Federal Government as plucking feathers from the eagle's tail. It (FIGURE 73) is captioned "The American Eagle in Danger," and Uncle Sam says, "What are you doing to that bird of mine. He doesn't belong to either of you. Look sharp, or he'll give you a taste of his claws!"

Two Currier and Ives cartoons of the

same year featured Uncle Sam in the colonial garb which had been used by some artists a generation earlier, except that in these he looks like Benjamin

Figure 73

Franklin. One (FIGURE 74), "Stephen Finding His Mother," shows Columbia punishing presidential candidate Stephen A. Douglas, as Uncle Sam encourages her: "That's right! Columbia, lay it on to him, for he richly deserves it, give him the Stripes till he sees Stars." The other (FIGURE 75), evidently done in prophetic vein during the campaign, has Uncle Sam taking down a sign that says: "WANTED — An honest, upright and capable man to take charge of this house for four years. Undoubted testimonials will be required. Apply to Uncle Sam, on the Premises." As the candidates appeal to him, he hands Lincoln a document: "This is to Certify

Figure 74 (below)

78

Figure 75

Figure 76 (below)

that I have hired A. Lincoln for four years from March 4th, 1861. U. Sam."

Until the forties Americans had been generally smooth-faced except for the frontiersmen who let their beards grow out of necessity and — in the winter — for warmth. Then the hirsute styles set by European royalty found their way to the other side of the Atlantic; the fops and dandies began to cultivate them. Sideburns, chin whiskers, and full beards were natural developments. Ironically, *Uncle Sam's Large Almanac for 1843* (FIGURE 76), published in Philadelphia, carried a piece of heavy satire titled "Moustaches," in which a rustic Yankee makes fun of such adornments. The irony consists in the fact that the time would come when Uncle Sam himself would be referred to in slang as "Mr. Whiskers."

9: Uncle Sam and Abe Lincoln

Though *Punch* had been first to publish a bearded Jonathan, and this several years before the onset of the Civil War, to Abraham Lincoln must be attributed the fact that this version stuck. After the war it became the standard and accepted likeness everywhere. As the struggle proceeded and British interests were ever more deeply involved, *Punch* used Jonathan less and Lincoln more, to represent the United States. Further, when Lincoln appeared he was usually dressed in the stars and stripes which had previously been reserved for Jonathan. To some degree American cartoonists did the same. Hence, when Nast and Keppler came to design their Uncle Sams in the postwar years, they chose to show him with a beard.

In allowing his beard to grow, Lincoln took the advice of a little girl, Grace Bedell, who wrote that she thought he would look better that way. And in so doing he also set a style. Aided by the beard, the artists of *Punch* and *London Fun* drew Lincoln as a sinister and saturnine character throughout the war. But even as they did so, they were helping to fix the bearded image of the United States. *Punch* devoted special attention to Lincoln in 1862, the year of Union setbacks. In July Lincoln is shown mixing the New York "Eye-Duster," a jibe at the press reports of the war (FIGURE 77). Early in August (FIGURE 78) he is trying to recruit Negro troops, and later that month (FIGURE 79) he is beset by lack of money and men. In September (FIGURE 80) a Confederate is presenting him with a promissory note: "I promise to subdue the South in 90 days — Abe Lincoln." This probably reflected the fact that some

THE LATEST FROM AMERICA;

Or, the New York "Eye-Duster," to be taken Every Day.

Figure 77

LINCOLN'S TWO DIFFICULTIES.

Lin. "WHAT? NO MONEY! NO MEN!"

Figure 79

Figure 78 (below)

ONE GOOD TURN DESERVES ANOTHER.

Old Abe. "WHY I DU DECLARE IT'S MY DEAR OLD FRIEND SAMBO! COURSE YOU'LL FIGHT FOR US, SAMBO. LEND US A HAND, OLD HOSS, DU!"

Figure 80 (below)

THE OVERDUE BILL.

Mr. South to Mr. North. "YOUR 'NINETY DAYS' PROMISSORY NOTE ISN'T TAKEN UP YET, SIRREE!"

81

YOU lay a wreath on murdered LINCOLN's
    bier
You, who with mocking pencil wont to
    trace,
Broad for the self-complacent British sneer,
His length of shambling limb, his furrowed
    face,

His gaunt, gnarled hands, his unkempt, bris-
    tling hair,
His garb uncouth, his bearing ill at ease,
His lack of all we prize as debonair,
Of power or will to shine, or art to please. . . .

Beside this corpse, that bears for winding-
    sheet
The Stars and Stripes he lived to rear anew,
Between the mourners at his head and feet,
Say, scurril-jester, is there room for *you?*

Yes, he had lived to shame me from my
    sneer,
To lame my pencil, and confute my pen —
To make me own this hind of princes peer,
This rail-splitter a true-born king of men.

Figure 81

ninety-day volunteers had been enrolled in the Union ranks; an old law provided that militia could not be made to serve more than three months in any one year.

In 1864 Tenniel comments sardonically on Lincoln's victory in his second election (FIGURE 81) by showing him as "The Federal Phoenix," rising out of the flames that devour the Constitution, commerce, free press, states rights, *habeas corpus,* and credit. It is hard to see, at this distance, why the British cartoonists remained so intransigent right to the end, unless perhaps the momentum gained by years of sniping allowed of no other attitude. With the death of Lincoln, *Punch* experienced feelings of remorse to which it gave vent in a long poem full of sorrow and self-accusation.

American cartoonists showed more versatility in their treatment of the war. In 1861 T. W. Strong published "The Schoolmaster Abroad" (FIGURE 82), in which a beardless Lincoln attired in stars and stripes is trying to coax the truant pupils out of the secession pool, as South Carolina, who has dropped the palmetto flag, bites him on the hand. A unique lithograph of this year (FIGURE 83) is "Uncle Sam Protecting His Property Against the Encroachments of His Cousin John." Uncle Sam, dressed as a Union officer, with Lincoln's face, is ejecting a uniformed John Bull from his garden as he holds a stick marked "Principles of Non-Interference." John Bull's boots are the Armstrongs guns being supplied by Britain to the forces of the South. Napoleon III crows from the fence, while

82

Figure 82
(above)

Figure 83

Beauregard and Jeff Davis are hanged in the background. This kind of wishful thinking permeates quite a few of the cartoons done in the early part of the war when many of the passionate partisans on both sides were sure that the conflict would be short, and that fitting punishment would soon be meted out to the dastardly leaders of the opposition.

In 1862 C. F. Morse drew a whole army of Jonathans (FIGURE 84) with the caption "Yankee Volunteers Marching into Dixie." This lithograph, the original in color, shows how definitely the costume had become associated with the cause of the North.

Neither Uncle Sam nor Jonathan appear in Confederate cartoons, which are, for the most part, diatribes against Lincoln and all his works. Indeed, the North Carolina *Standard* of June 1, 1861, somewhat prematurely, sought to lay the old gentleman to rest:

OBITUARY OF UNCLE SAM

"That good old soul, we ne'er shall see him more." . . . the subject of our notice was of English origin, his father being the celebrated John Bull . . . Uncle Sam was a great land-speculator, and acquired immense farms in the West and South, which he distributed with very little regard to equity, adaptation or pursuit. Many of his children resided in the South, and found out, by actual experiment, that they could not work their lands to advantage themselves; they therefore purchased negroes, and found that they could work their lands to the advantage of both. But Uncle Sam, under the dictation

Figure 85

of his Northern children, resisted this natural, profitable and benevolent system of cultivation, excluded slaves from a part of the common land, attempted to drive them away from another, and actually went so far as to say that he would not allow them to be used on the old farms, which his Southern children had not got from him, but by fee simple title, from their grandfather, John Bull. . . . These domestic troubles had their logical effect on the old man's constitution . . . he elected one Abraham Lincoln, a creature of his Northern children, to be overseer of his *whole* domain. This was a great insult . . . Lincoln gave an order for 75,000 assistants to join him, for the purpose of whipping his Southern brethren into strict submission. . . . This prospect of brethren shedding each others' blood was too much for Uncle Sam to bear. . . . He died the very day the bloody order was issued. . . . It may be gratifying to the surviving friends of

Uncle Sam, to learn that the most of his Southern children have appointed the Hon. Jeff Davis overseer, and declare their intention, with his assistance, to wrest the old family mansion from its present vulgar occupants. . . .

A Currier and Ives lithograph signed "Ben Day" appeared in 1864 (FIGURE 85) with the caption "Caving in, or a Rebel 'Deeply Humiliated.' " It is a prize fight between Lincoln and Davis, the former clearly ahead. Lincoln wears the colors of the United States, as in the British cartoons. The boxing match was for many years a favorite device for showing antagonists in action, as were various other sports, matches, and games.

85

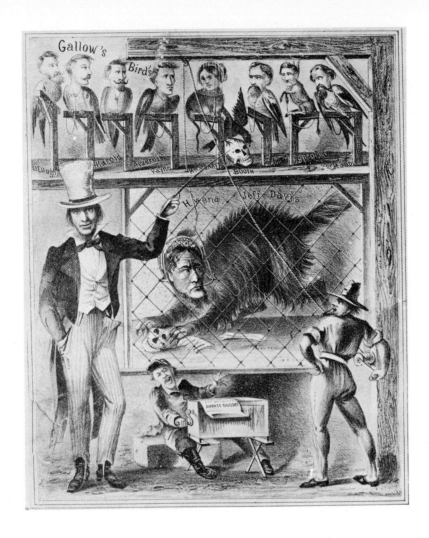

Figure 86

After victory, the Northern artists lost no opportunity to gloat. An entry of June, 1865, titled "Uncle Sam's Menagerie," features a caged Jeff Davis, and the "Gallow's Birds" connected with the plot on Lincoln's life. In the foreground, a man plays "Yankee Doodle" on a hand organ (FIGURE 86).

This marks one of the last appearances of a beardless Uncle Sam. The bearded image of Lincoln as the champion of the Union had been etched so deeply in men's minds that it was retained in later cartoons. During the Civil War the popularity of *Harper's* and *Leslie's*, as well as a number of other periodicals such as *Vanity Fair* and *Punchinello*, had kept the caricatured figure of Lincoln before the public, and in so doing had also helped to doom the separately published cartoon. From this time on, the political cartoonist drew for the public journals.

10: The Era of Nast

Just as Harriet Beecher Stowe with her *Uncle Tom's Cabin* was considered by Lincoln to have been one of those largely responsible for bringing on the Civil War, so Thomas Nast was credited by him with having helped mightily to win it. "Thomas Nast has been our best recruiting sergeant," said Lincoln near the end of the war. "His emblematic cartoons have never failed to arouse enthusiasm and patriotism, and have always seemed to come just when those articles were getting scarce." Similarly, when General Grant was asked who was the foremost figure in civil life developed by the rebellion, he replied, "I think, Thomas Nast. He did as much as any one man to preserve the Union and bring the war to an end."

Born in Germany in 1840, Nast came to the United States as a boy of six. He showed early promise, and was doing sketches for *Leslie's Weekly* at the age of fifteen. He covered news events for the most part until he joined the staff of *Harper's Weekly* in 1862. He did not find Harper's studio congenial, preferring to work at home. He drew so quickly and well that he was used by Fletcher Harper as an example to the rest of the staff. Nast had firm convictions, and these he ex-had firm convictions, and these he expressed in his pictures, which sometimes contained as many words as an editorial. Fletcher Harper learned to give his star free rein, assured that whatever he drew would appeal to a big and growing audience. Then in 1863 Nast began to turn out the semiallegorical drawings which established him as America's foremost pictorial journalist. After the war he turned to political cartoons, and it was his relentless pursuit of the Tweed Ring which was credited with the final overthrow of that cynical pack of municipal pirates.

Best known of all Nast's cartoons

(1877) was "The Tammany Tiger Loose" in the arena, devouring law and justice as Boss Tweed and his minions look on (FIGURE 87). This was the first use of a symbol that became a permanent fixture. As much as any single influence, this cartoon galvanized the forces of decency and toppled the rotten structure of the plunderbund.

At the peak of his powers, Nast was such a well-known personality that he often drew cartoons in which he was a principal character himself. No other American cartoonist, and probably no other in any country — not even Daumier — has ever wielded such influence on his times. Hence, it was natural that when Nast decided to use Uncle Sam, which he did repeatedly in the seventies and eighties, his rendition would stand as definitive.

It is interesting that Nast early depicted Uncle Sam as concerned by the agitation of communism in America. This is shown (FIGURE 88) by a drawing of March, 1874, captioned "A Foreign and Poisonous Weed." Communism is represented as a big toadstool, about to be chopped out by the Granger, who is watched and applauded by Uncle Sam. The communists had tried to infiltrate the biggest organization of American farmers, with whom they never had much success. Thereafter the communists turned their attention to the infant labor movement, which in time was to find them a formidable threat.

Nast was fond of showing Uncle Sam and Columbia together. Often she is lecturing him about his shortcomings. Such is "Giving U. S. Hail Columbia," published in 1878. Here (FIGURE 89) she takes him to task for his financial instability, as evidenced by increased coinage

Figure 87

Figure 88

Figure 89

of silver dollars. Be it noted that Columbia's costume is in keeping with the then current style, whereas Uncle Sam's outfit is the old familiar. Nast preferred plain waistcoat and hat, though he did sometimes sprinkle a few stars on the waistcoat and stripes on the collar.

Nast was often caricatured himself in rival publications and denounced in their editorials. Hence, his large public noticed at once when he failed to treat a significant personage or event, and began to wonder why. Such was the case with the Hayes Administration. By 1877, Nast's high hopes had changed to disappointment. He vigorously opposed Hayes's announced intention to pacify the white South by removing all military protection from the Negro voter, and refused to refer to the President except in an unfavorable way. Fletcher Harper had died in 1876, and the new publisher, J. W. Harper, Jr., was inclined to side with the editor, George William Curtis, who favored paci-

fication. Letters poured in asking for some indication of Nast's point of view. Nast was ready to answer them with a drawing and told Harper as much. According to Albert Bigelow Paine, the following conversation ensued:

"But you want to attack the President, Nast. We want to give him a chance. We believe he means well."

"He means well but he doesn't do well," retorted Nast.

"But that's just your opinion. The general disposition seems to be to stand back and give the President's policy a chance."

"Will you let me put that in the form of a cartoon?"

"Yes, if you keep Hayes out of it."[1]

Nast accomplished this miracle in as neat a *tour de force* as has ever been put into a cartoon. He drew himself, sitting in the policy chair in the Blue Room of the White House. Uncle Sam holds him there, as he says, "Our artist must keep cool, and sit down, and see how it works." On the wall is a "Public Notice: Watch

Figure 90

Figure 90

Figure 91

and Pray — Stand Back and Give the President's Policy a Chance. (Signed) Gen. Disposition." This cartoon (FIGURE 90) created such a stir that Nast drew a sequel to it (FIGURE 91), with the bottom dropping out of the policy chair. "Our patient artist" falls through, holding a pair of scissors high in token of defiance, as Uncle Sam flees through the door of the Blue Room. As usual, the wall editorializes.

Nast is usually, and erroneously, credited with the first depiction of the Republican elephant, in a cartoon which appeared in *Harper's Weekly* on November 7, 1874 (FIGURE 92). The somewhat inflated beast was supposed to represent the huge size of the G.O.P. congressional vote that year.

Two years later he used it to good effect in the disputed Hayes-Tilden election. In "The Elephant Walks Around" (FIGURE

93) he shows the massive beast, with a load of school children riding and Uncle Sam as mahout, trampling on a double-headed Tammany tiger bearing the likeness of Tilden and Hendricks, the Democratic candidates.

Actually, the Republican elephant dates back almost to the beginning of the party. It was first used in 1860 during Lincoln's campaign. On August 9 of that year the *Illinois State Journal* announced a political rally with a dynamic pachyderm wearing boots and running full speed (FIGURE 94). A sign on his blanket said, "Clear the Track," while "We Are Coming" floated between trunk and tail. Other headlines beneath cried, "A Political Earthquake" and "The Prairies on Fire for Lincoln."

The particular running elephant used was a printer's cut of a kind which was kept ready to hand for illustrative pur-

Figure 92

Figure 93 (below)

Figure 94 (below)

A Political Earthquake!

THE PRAIRIES ON FIRE FOR LINCOLN!

THE BIGGEST DEMONSTRATION EVER HELD IN THE WEST!

Figure 95

poses in job printing. Whether Nast ever saw this is problematical.

While the printer's cut of 1860 was the first G. O. P. elephant, another elephant appeared as early as 1832 to represent the opposition to a Democratic president. This was in an anonymous print, "Congressional Elephant, or Last Desperate Pull for Power." It shows Andrew Jackson, encouraged by Major Downing, pulling the elephant's tail, while Liberty (or Columbia) rides on his trunk. Here the elephant stands for the Clay forces in the pitched battle over the Bank of the United States (FIGURE 95).

The elephant figures often in the early symbolism of California. During the years preceding the Civil War, the phrase "see the elephant" was much used to mean experience of some great event, and it was so used by veteran soldiers to recruits during the war, to prepare them for their first encounters with the enemy.

By 1862 the elephant had been accepted to such a degree that it was being used even by the anti-Lincoln press. Here, of course, it became a symbol of Lincoln's "tyranny."

The elephant had long been used to represent the idea of power and size. The Romans put it on coins struck in 275 B.C. to commemorate a victory over Pyrrhus. After America was discovered, artists sometimes used the elephant to denote the West as well as the East Indies.

Nast has also been credited with the origin of the Democratic donkey, and he did give it the form in which it appears today (FIGURE 96). But this, too, goes back a good bit further. For generations the jackass had been known as the poor man's animal. Since Bible times he had

Figure 96

patiently borne the burdens of the world. Franklin made a point of this during the debate on the rights of suffrage during the Constitutional Convention. To those who wished to restrict suffrage to property holders, Franklin asked, What of the farmer who came to town to vote? And what if, on the way, his donkey died. Then the farmer, who had lost his property, would also have lost his right to vote. In that case, Franklin concluded, who actually had the right to vote, the man or the donkey? This helped to kill the qualification, but even so, most of the states did maintain some such property requirements until the triumph of Jacksonian democracy in the 1830's. At this time many of the new voters were illiterate. But they could all understand the cartoon, which was widely and effectively used. And just as Yankee Doodle had often been represented as riding on a pony, Jackson, widely billed as the poor

man's friend, usually appeared on a donkey.

Jackson's opponents, the Whigs, tried to give visible form to the legendary animal, half horse and half alligator, which began in the boastings of the Ohio River boatmen, who declared they were so composed. This failed to strike a responsive chord in the rest of the country, however, and was soon abandoned. In 1840, William Henry Harrison's hard cider, log cabin, and coonskin cap won a big following — so much so that the raccoon fought it out with the donkey until the Civil War. Of recent years the raccoon cap has enjoyed renewed popularity, thanks to Senator Estes Kefauver and Davy Crockett.

Later party symbols have also proved ephemeral. The bull moose, taken as the sign of Theodore Roosevelt's split-off from the Republican Party in 1912, died about as soon as Bull Moose party sentiment did. Again this massive animal stood for power and a certain regal quality which was doubtless intended to be memorable. Those who knew T. R. best could never understand why he had chosen such an emblem, since while he was known as a doughty huntsman, he had never had much luck with moose.

Another practice begun during Jackson's administration — the use of human heads on the bodies of animals — sometimes went to incredible lengths. The animals chosen were all too often skunks, pigs, weasels, and rats. Defamation reached extremes which no publication would ever sanction today. Yet it flourished for decades, finding particular popularity in the state of Pennsylvania. There the animal-human combinations became so scurrilous

Figure 97

cian," characterized by Nast in 1886 as "the curse of our country" (FIGURE 97). Holding a scepter made of a ballot box, he vaunts the triumph of the spoils system over decent government. This character was adopted by many other cartoonists as the archetype of the politico.

Nast's great days were coming to a close. He was about to pass the mantle of America's leading cartoonist to Joseph Keppler, for eighteen years a mainstay of *Puck,* the humorous weekly which had been founded in 1877. Fred Opper, long a member of the *Puck* staff, was responsible for a cartoon which appeared in that journal, in which Nast and Keppler kneel in supplication to Death, the Grim Destroyer, who had removed so many of their best subjects. Opper called it: "Rough on America's Great Cartoonists."

W. A. Rogers in his reminiscences says of Nast: "To have the skin cut off one's back was bad enough, but to be made ridiculous besides — that is what made Nast's satire so deadly." Although it may be a subject for debate as to whether Thomas Nast drew the best pictures of Uncle Sam ever published, this much is sure: Nast, more than any other artist, was responsible for the Uncle Sam who appears daily on the editorial pages of the nation's press, and indeed, the publications of the whole world.

that Senator Boies Penrose, when Republican leader of the state during the early 1900's, managed to get the legislature to pass a law prohibiting them.

Nast invented what is called today "the running gag" — a recurrent theme or personality that serves to knit together a series of cartoons on the same general subject. Such were the rapscallion members of the Tweed Ring, the Tammany tiger, the rag baby of inflation, and other characters to which Nast gave the first full expression.

These included "The Practical Politi-

94

11: Uncle Sam's Progress

For the past century Uncle Sam in his visible form has taken the leading role in every notable event of American history How well or how ill he has played his part has depended to a considerable degree on the viewpoints and the abilities of the artists who have used him to mirror their times. The ascendancy of Uncle Sam as a cartoon character really began in the seventies.

Everything was growing bigger and moving faster in America, and since Uncle Sam had always been a mover and a boomer, he went along with progress, though perhaps not without a nostalgic pang for the old, leisurely times when it took a week to go by coach from Washington to Boston, and the European news was five weeks old when it reached us. Now we had steamships and ocean cables, and some people were even talking about

flying machines, though of course that was sheer lunacy. Certain it was, though, that the remote corners of the globe were moving in on us, and we were having to adjust our national policies to meet such developments. As early as 1875 Frank Bellew recognized this with a prophetic cartoon (FIGURE 98): "The Two Young Giants — Ivan and Jonathan reaching for Asia by Opposite Routes." When this ran in *Harper's Weekly*, the United States was concluding a commercial agreement with Hawaii. Russia, meanwhile, was pushing down from Siberia into Mongolia. Bellew, an Englishman, evidently preferred to follow the lead of *Punch* and show a beardless Jonathan rather than a bearded Uncle Sam, which by that time had become virtually standard with American cartoonists.

In the front rank of those who became the delineators of the new bearded Uncle

Sam, as developed by Nast, was Joseph Keppler, an Austrian immigrant who had arrived in America in 1868. He had been trained for the theater in Vienna, and pursued such activities in St. Louis the first year after his arrival. He then launched several comic papers, none of which lived long. Meanwhile he sold cartoons to other magazines. Not until he founded *Puck* nine years after his arrival did he hit upon the right formula to win and hold public favor.

Typical of the Uncle Sam that helped to build Keppler's renown is the cartoon (FIGURE 99) from an 1880 issue of *Puck* with the cut line "Welcome to All." Done in the year of the Garfield-Hancock election, this shows immigrants from Europe entering the "U. S. Ark of Refuge" to escape taxes, kings, military training, and dungeons. Aimed at the foreign-born vote, this was considered to be a tribute to the Republicans who had made it possible. Keppler's Uncle Sam is potbellied and looks rather like a German music hall comedian of that era.

In 1887 C. G. Bush drew "Uncle Sam

Figure 98

Figure 99

Figure 100

and His Doctors," which is notable mainly because it updates the original situation in which Uncle Sam had been first depicted back in the early thirties (FIGURE 100). His doctors (Congressmen John G. Carlisle and S. J. Randall) are prescribing for him again, and although his maladies are different, the prognosis is gloomy as usual.

Bush was known as a cultivated gentleman with a fine sense of humor. He was one of the first to draw a daily cartoon, which required a different technique from that of the complex, crowded drawings of earlier times. He became a master of the swift summing up which delivers the point in a flash. Such cartoons had to be drawn quickly, often with the presses waiting. This favored more frequent use of symbols understood by everybody; therefore the wide use of Uncle Sam, as well as the elephant and the donkey, to crystallize an idea.

Fred Opper, like Nast, sometimes dressed Uncle Sam in costumes other than the usual one. In "Obstructing the Public Highway" (FIGURE 101), he is garbed as a policeman, in which capacity he is ordering the Republican peddler James G. Blaine off the street because his license is no good.[1] In a window in the background, Whitelaw Reid of the New York

Figure 101

Tribune is represented as in charge of the "Private Bureau of Permits for Political Nuisances." Opper was to have a long and fruitful career, but despite his many attainments as a political cartoonist, he will be most fondly remembered by many devotees of the comic strip in the first third of the twentieth century as the creator of Happy Hooligan, as well as Alphonse and Gaston.

That the growth of antimonopoly sentiment was slow but sure is demonstrated in a cartoon by W. A. Rogers from an 1888 *Harper's:* "A Huge Feeder But a Poor Milker" (FIGURE 102). Columbia milks the multiheaded creature "Monopoly" as Uncle Sam says, "If the beast cannot yield enough to fill that little pail, the sooner my stable is quit of her, the better." Rogers used this graphic metaphor again and again, in the Nast tradi-

tion. He believed that humor was not absolutely essential to political cartoons, and strove instead to make an impression through sheer imaginative power. Rogers' Uncle Sams are slimmer and less grotesque than the Keppler versions; they radiate an air of capability and no-nonsense.

A "regular" in *Puck* at the turn of the century was J. S. Pughe, who drew Uncle Sam with the forehead of a philosopher and clothes obviously hand-tailored. One Pughe drawing (FIGURE 103) uses Uncle Sam to graph the American credo regarding the practicability of socialism. With copybook simplicity it shows that if all the wealth of the country were to be divided up equally among all the people, the thrifty and resourceful businessman, who looks more than a trace like John D. Rockefeller, would in a short time have

98

Figure 102

Figure 103
(below)

his share and the socialist's, too. "The Socialists' Theory and How It Would Work Out" was doubtless framed in many a business office and shown to many a young hothead to disprove his theories of how to share the wealth and make every man a king.

Homer Davenport was the leading cartoonist developed by the Hearst newspapers during the nineties. As such, his

Figure 104

work exerted a powerful effect on the molding of national opinion. Davenport was a simple country lad, who seemed to those with whom he worked to have few ideas and almost no sophistication. Yet his cartoons have a bite that indicates the degree of this talent. He drew a remarkable sequence of Uncle Sams which achieved wide popularity at the time of the Spanish-American War; so much so that they were later published separately.

In "Getting the Old Gun Ready" (FIG-URE 104) the artist notes the truculent attitude taken by President Cleveland in 1895 toward the boundary dispute between Venezuela and British Guiana — an argument which was at length settled amicably.

Uncle Sam soon came to realize that his overseas adventures had produced problems as well as glory. But he is facing them resolutely in Louis Dalrymple's cartoon from *Puck* with the title "UNCLE SAM'S Picnic" (FIGURE 105). As he loads his new possessions onto the wagon, "Old Man Monroe Doctrine" asks him, "Ain't ye takin' too many, Sam?" To this he replies, "No, Gran'pa, I reckon this team will be strong enough for them all!" Dalrymple joined the staff of *Puck* in the eighties and did some of their best work. He was known for his keen political sense and ability to get at the essence of a situation graphically.

Uncle Sam was learning what it meant to represent power in the modern world.

100

Figure 105

Figure 106 (below)

In the Mexican crisis of 1916, he — and the American people — had a brief advance notice of the problems which were to vex the country through the years ahead. The Marines landed at Vera Cruz, and Black Jack Pershing pursued evasive bandits through the arid wastes of the border country. Two years earlier the Austrian Archduke had been assassinated at Sarajevo, and suddenly the troubles of Europe had become Uncle Sam's problems, too. In *Punch,* F. H. Townsend shows him at his desk in September, 1914 (FIGURE 106). The German imperial dachshund sits up and begs for his attention as he lights a stogie over the caption "Nothing doing." The pro-German sentiment in America was loud and strong, and did its best to drown out the adherents of

101

Figure 107

Figure 111

Figure 108

the Allied Powers. For nearly three years the papers were full of harried Uncle Sams trying to put out the sparks from a world on fire. Plagued by secret agents, diplomatic insolence, U-boat sinkings, and Allied nagging, Uncle Sam was pictured by turns as aghast, angry, and deluded.

During this period of uneasy neutrality, the New York *Evening World*'s artist John Cassell took a grim view of the enemy at home in a cartoon (FIGURE 107) captioned "Over there — Over here!" As Uncle Sam watches the fighting overseas, an alien prepares to knife him in the back. Such accusations made life extremely uncomfortable for many loyal Americans of German extraction, whose every word and move became suspect, especially after America entered the war.

The Germans themselves saw Uncle Sam as a disagreeable old buttinsky. The magazine *Kladderadatsch* evoked his alarm at the near approach of the U-boats to his shores (FIGURE 108). Uncle looks like Ichabod Crane, and for the first time on record, he wears striped socks.

Now came James Montgomery Flagg

Figure 109

Figure 110

with the best-known and most widely distributed Uncle Sam ever drawn — the famous 1917 recruiting poster "I Want You for U. S. Army." So compelling is this design (FIGURE 109), and so insistent the pointing finger, that the picture has been recalled to service again and again. It was particularly effective in the poster medium for which it was intended; the eyes seemed to follow the passer-by and bore into his back. This poster was probably adapted from one featuring General Kitchener in a similar pose which had been used successfully in Britain early in World War I (FIGURE 110).

In Europe the leading cartoonist developed by the war was the Belgian Louis Raemakers, who had first made his reputation with a drawing of a Belgian father shaking his fist at the Zeppelin which dropped the bomb that killed his child. Raemakers drew a powerful series of Uncle Sams which were widely used for propaganda purposes. One has a two-gun Uncle forcing the Kaiser to open up his bag of loot from the countries he has despoiled (FIGURE 111).

After America's war effort was really rolling, the cartoon crop developed a sameness that militated against original concepts. This was partially conditioned by the Bureau of Cartoons, which, under the auspices of George Creel's Committee on Public Information, published a weekly *Bulletin for Cartoonists*. It advised the artists where they could be of greatest service in supporting the war effort, whether it was selling Liberty bonds, saving fuel, or cultivating a war garden. When they had done their duty in these

Figure 112

began to find fault with their deliverers. Uncle Sam's cherished ideals were washed down the drain at Versailles, and his erstwhile friends and allies called him "Uncle Shylock" when he happened to mention the little matter of the war debts they owed him. It seemed to be everybody for himself and the devil take the hindmost. Disgusted and bitter, Uncle Sam retreated into his shell of isolation again. And yet, even as he repeated over again the words of Washington advising against entangling alliances, he knew in his heart that the world had closed around him and was looking to him. What Uncle had yet to learn was the wry wisdom of John Bull — that it is more important for a world leader to do a good job than to be loved for it.

Uncle Sam's initial reaction was expressed by William Ireland in the Columbus *Dispatch* (FIGURE 113). In the top picture he is shown leaping into the water to

areas, most of the cartoonists went back to berating the Kaiser, who lent himself so well to that sort of thing. Hanging him in one way or another was a favorite method of doing this. Even Charles Dana Gibson succumbed to the lure of helmet and hemp (FIGURE 112). Wilhelm, shown with bloody hands, is about to be strung up by a shirt-sleeved Uncle Sam, as punishment for the destruction he has wreaked on the world. Like Raemakers, Gibson shows his warlike Uncle Sam with boots on and coatless. The delicate lines cultivated by the creator of the Gibson girls are entirely absent.

The United States had rolled to victory on a wave of idealistic fervor. But it is not in the nature of man to sustain such exalted moods indefinitely. The French crowds which had welcomed the first American troops with *"Vive* Sammee!" and which had saluted Wilson as a savior,

Figure 113 (below)

rescue drowning Europe. But when the
damsel embraces him and cries "Marry
me!" as a cleric approaches on a dead run
bearing the Covenant of the League of
Nations, Uncle is taken aback. Hence the
caption: "It's so Sudden — We'd Like a
Little Time to Think It Over."

In a state of dreadful uncertainty,
Uncle Sam let the "little group of willful
men" shut the door on the League of
Nations, and thereby set the stage for another world cataclysm. The new freedom
was replaced by the normalcy of Warren
G. Harding, whose credo consisted of a
set of pious platitudes. Daniel Fitzpatrick
highlighted one of these in the St. Louis
Post-Dispatch (FIGURE 114). In a holier-
than-thou pose, Uncle is enhaloed by one
of Harding's avowed goals: "An America
That Will Reform the World." The artist
has him saying, "I thank thee that I am
not as other men are." Such false and un-
realistic attitudes keyed the decade which

Figure 115

Figure 114 (below)

has been called the Era of Wonderful
Nonsense. Uncle was mainly occupied
with greetings to transatlantic fliers and
channel swimmers. In 1928 Norman
Rockwell painted Uncle on a *Saturday
Evening Post* front cover in a state of full
flight (FIGURE 115). Probably nobody else
could have done it quite as well. For it is
Rockwell's genius, in which he is unique
among all American illustrato s, that he
can evoke the essential beauty of the familiar in such a way as to make it significant and memorable.

Rollin Kirby's Prohibition bluenose led
raids on beer flats, and everybody who
could scrape a couple of dollars together
was buying stocks and getting rich on
paper. Waves of foreign lecturers landed

105

Figure 116

on our shores, told us how barbaric we were to worship the golden calf, and departed with their wallets considerably enriched. Americans accepted these reproofs meekly, feeling that such flagellation was probably warranted. Had not their Puritan grandsires mortified the flesh? And just as such practices had cleared the way for the golden era of New England culture, so perhaps the patience of the ladies' clubs under the lashes of foreign lecturers might foreshadow a new American renaissance. But not all agreed. Some thought the advisers from overseas were blabbermouths and busybodies who would have done better to stay home and mind their own affairs. This viewpoint is reflected in a cartoon by Albert T. Reid (FIGURE 116).

Figure 117 (below)

Figure 118 (below)

106

Figure 119

A somber Uncle Sam marches like Gulliver through a cloud of Lilliputian lecturers, each of whom is trying to direct him in the way he should go. Says the cartoonist: "It is his own fault if he gets lost."

In some quarters the nationalistic spirit was expressed by efforts to pass more stringent immigration laws, and by a recrudescence of the racist antiforeignism which had risen periodically in American history to twist and inflame men's minds. One evidence of this was the Ku Klux Klan, with its cross burnings, Klaverns, Konclaves, and Kleagles. At first this organization seemed sinister enough, but when the members were ordered by the Imperial Wizard to unmask, what appeared was perhaps more cause for laughter than fear. Edmund Duffy used this for the theme of his cartoon "Put It On Again!" in which Uncle Sam indicates that he understands now why the K.K.K.

used masks in the first place (FIGURE 117). "Ding" (J. N. Darling) of the New York *Herald Tribune* took more of a comic artist approach; he showed an Uncle Sam who was quite human and vulnerable, and who loved his creature comforts. This emerges from a 1932 cartoon of Uncle Sam and John Bull being asked for a disarmament contribution, to which both are politely oblivious (FIGURE 118).

One of the best-known cartoonists of the early thirties was Percy L. Crosby, whose "Skippy" had been very successful as a comic strip. Crosby obviously felt deeply on such issues as national defense, and this comes through, just as it had in Nast's work on the same subject. Crosby's style was crisp and full of contrast; his situations supercharged with dramatic impact — sometimes almost too much. His cartoons were published in the Washington *Herald*. The one reproduced (FIGURE 119) appeared in 1933, and commented

Figure 121 (below)   Figure 120

since 1927, when he began work on the London *Star,* has been David Low. A New Zealander, Low drew for papers there and in Australia before leaving for Britain, where he was for years the mainstay of Lord Beaverbrook's *Daily Express.* Later he joined the Laborite *Daily Herald.* Today Low is ranked by many authorities as the world's leading cartoonist.

By 1937 Low was concerned with the American Neutrality Act, which forbade Americans to ship goods or lend money to belligerent powers. "Uncle Sam's Bomb-Proof Shelter" (FIGURE 120) is being inspected by a dubious President Roosevelt and Secretary of State Cordell Hull, as the Senate pastes on new layers of neutrality speeches. The shelter is labeled "Purely Negative Policy."

For many years Edwin Marcus of the

bitterly on the current cut in defense funds. This has been a prime target for cartoonists through the years.

Uncle Sam's chief British delineator

108

Figure 122

Figure 23 (below)

New York Times has drawn Uncle Sams of dignity and power. Typical is "Better take a look at my union card," done in 1939, when Government workers were threatening to strike (FIGURE 121).

Naturalism keys the work of the Washington Star's Jim Berryman, who shows candidates Roosevelt, Truman, Dewey, and Bricker at work on the jigsaw puzzle of the 1944 election, as an Uncle Sam resembling a country storekeeper cautions them (FIGURE 122), "I know you boys are tired, but by Wednesday morning I want the whole thing straightened out!"

Distortions of the Uncle Sam image have been employed frequently to indi-

The Worldly Hope men set their Hearts upon
Turns Ashes—or it prospers; and anon,
Like Snow upon the Desert's dusty Face,
Lighting a little hour or two—is gone.
                              Omar Khayyám

U.S.

GENEVA

BERLIN

POTSDAM
YALTA

Figure 124

cate the tenor of world opinion and our own reactions to it. Such is the inflated figure in Fred Seibel's cartoon of 1948 in the Richmond *Times-Dispatch* (FIGURE 123). Captioned "How he looks to the world at large," the ballooning Uncle appears neither friendly nor comfortable.

The deepening mood of disillusionment after World War II is summed up swiftly in a New York *Daily News* cartoon by G. C. Batchelor (FIGURE 124). Uncle Sam broods upon the lost hopes of the postwar conferences, and his discouragement is caught in a fateful quotation from Omar Khayyám on the transience of human plans.

110

12: The Jaundiced-Eye View

Throughout the nineteenth century Uncle Sam became well known to peoples overseas as the proprietor of the Land of Promise. If American streets were not paved with gold, at least the common man could with reasonable exertion hope to hew out a future here much better than any he had known in his homeland. Millions of them proved it, and the news of their achievements went abroad. The cornucopia of plenty over which Uncle presided seemed to be bottomless. As American prosperity grew apace, the rest of the world watched curiously and sought to explain this phenomenon. It obeyed none of the rules of the past. There was no hereditary aristocracy, no carefully guarded transmission of power, no laws to prevent the artisan from becoming a capitalist. With Uncle Sam all things were possible.

Human nature being what it is, this utopia was just a little too much for foreign visitors to swallow. Charles Dickens led the long procession of travelers from afar who found serpents in paradise. As for Americans, they were humbly conscious of their cultural shortcomings and only too eager to pay tribute to foreign pundits who expounded at length on the subject. Uncle Sam was painted as an uncouth dollar-chaser, a stereotype which persisted long after American collectors had brought a good share of Europe's art to this country, nearly every major city had its own symphony orchestra, and many of them were actively supporting community theaters. Few critics found time to comment on the growth of both public and private education and the widespread encouragement of the free library.

Figure 125

The Uncle Sam image had thus long been the butt of ridicule, sometimes friendly, sometimes not. But it remained for the communists to use the symbol of the envied United States for the kind of hate propaganda in which they excel.

Since the Russians generally outspend us in propaganda, their distortions of Uncle Sam and his motives have often been singularly effective. Americans, on the other hand, have viewed such efforts as not quite honorable. In the war of ideas we spend more than 400 times as much on arms as we do on the projection of our principles to peoples overseas. The results can be seen in the cartoons downgrading Uncle Sam that appear in many parts of the world.

The communist propagandists are learned in the lore of symbolism: they

Figure 126 (below)

Hence, when Uncle Sam began to assume a position of power in world affairs, doubts were expressed as to his fitness for such a mission. This was mirrored in a cartoon run by the German *Kladderadatsch* in 1903 (FIGURE 125), in which a gawky Uncle Sam, mostly knees and elbows, wearing a flat hat and smoking a pipe, is the cynosure of all eyes. This, says the caption, is "what we may expect in the year of grace 1920. The streets of Berlin are no longer cleared for empty court carriages, but for Uncle Sam, who rides through them on his golden calf." Little did the cartoonist know how prophetic these words were to be.

Recent years have produced many foreign commentaries, all more or less critical. Typical is *La Case de L'Oncle Sam,* by Henri Troyat, in which our folkways are examined with more understanding than is usually apparent (FIGURE 126).

Figure 127

early seized upon Uncle Sam as a prime exemplar of the evils of capitalism. He is usually depicted as the fiendishly clever mastermind of a criminal gang whose only interests are profits however made and plunder wherever stolen.

Foremost stirrer of this witches' brew is the Soviet "humor" magazine *Krokodil,* from the pages of which come several of the examples reproduced herewith. The first (FIGURE 127), "Philanthropic Uncle Sam," dates from 1939. He is saying, "I'd be happy to sell you armaments. But I beg you, please don't hurt anybody with them." Arms are advertised on the placard in back. The one on the counter says, "Credit spoils friendship."

On a more somber note, Uncle Sam stands at John Bull's bedside in a cartoon of 1940 (FIGURE 128) and says, "He has to live! He owes me so much!"

Such themes, designed to split the unity of the West so that its elements can be

dealt with piecemeal, are fundamental with the Kremlin mouthpieces. *Krokodil*'s fulminations against the United States were especially virulent during the period of the Nazi-Soviet nonaggression pact, signed in August, 1939, and violated by Hitler in June, 1941, with his invasion of Russia. However, no sooner had this event occurred than the entire Soviet propaganda apparatus turned off the anti-Western tirades and turned on paeans of praise and comradeship, meanwhile delving into the beast and butcher category to find names terrible enough for the Nazis.

But this period of mutual toleration, if not understanding, ended almost as abruptly as it began. With victory, the old hostilities were reasserted. Soon the hounds of Agitprop were baying on the old scents.

Figure 128 (below)

Figure 129

Figure 130

Figure 131 (below)   Figure 132 (below)

114

The perennial effort to sow dissension between Britain and America is displayed in another cartoon which shows a purse-proud Uncle Sam surveying a map of his ally and reaching for his wallet (FIGURE 129). This caption: "It's all mine," says the dollar. "Tell me, please, how much do you want for this second-hand island?" Uncle wears a wing collar!

In similar vein is another in the divide-and-conquer series, in which Uncle Sam, in formal dress, is punching a hole in the belt of an unkempt and woebegone John Bull. The sardonic title is: "American Aid to Britain" (FIGURE 130).

When cartoonists are forced to pluck the same string again and again, it is hard to find variations. Few of the graphic thrusts at Uncle Sam in *Krokodil* are very adroit. A sample of the kind of heavy-handed work that fills its pages is seen in the human pyramid labeled "Equal Partners" (FIGURE 131). This time Uncle Sam wears tattersall trousers, which the Soviet cartoonists seem to find more corrupt than stripes. The Russians are also unique in showing a spectacled Uncle Sam, which probably derives from the stereotype of the average American wearing horn-rimmed glasses. The spectacles are drawn so as to produce a cold and calculating look, thus accentuating the sinister effect.

Western humor magazines are inclined to laugh at such attempts, but not for the reasons intended. For example, *Punch* distilled the "line" in one devastating take-off by Sillince that appeared in 1951 (FIGURE 132).

The Soviet satellite press also takes regular flings at Uncle Sam, though not with the single-minded efficiency of the

Figure 133

Russians. *Ludas Matyi,* a cartoon sheet published in Budapest, depicts a multi-armed Uncle Sam under the caption "American Siva in South Asia" (FIGURE 133). One hand holds "military commitments," another grasps "pacts." The line beneath says, "I cannot give you freedom and liberty because every hand is full."

Another labeled "Main USA Policy After Paris" shows a mean-visaged Uncle Sam attempting atom bomb diplomacy, in which he is spurned by Paris and welcomed by Bonn (FIGURE 134).

Hardly less bitter are the versions of Uncle Sam which appear in the press of more friendly nations. For instance, a Latin-American effort attempts to demonstrate the errors in his Good Neighbor policy (FIGURE 135). And an Egyptian cartoon (FIGURE 136) shows him, with John Bull, providing Israel with "arms for the sake of peace."

Similarly, Italy's *Candido* re-enacts "St. George and the Dragon," with Uncle Sam thrown from the back of a skittish Tito, frightened by the malignant look of the Soviet dragon (FIGURE 137).

In the newspapers of India and Asia

115

Az USA súlypontpolitikája Párizs után...

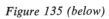

Figure 134

Figure 136 (below)

Figure 135 (below)

116

Figure 137

Figure 138 (below)

generally, Uncle fares according to the political view of the editors. An imaginative, though not very well drawn, example appeared in Bangalore's *Deccan Herald* in 1955 (FIGURE 138). Union Health Minister Kaur had recently returned to India after a tour of China, and had proposed a campaign against the fly menace as he had seen it in operation there. "Anti-Fly Campaign" shows the campaign in full swing, but the flies are insect Uncle Sams.

Another from a vernacular paper, the Tamil daily *Swadesamitran,* shows Uncle Sam and other Western powers enjoying themselves as they hurl knives at and through their Indian victim (FIGURE 139). Above his head appears the caption "U. N. Charter," while the three knives that have hit him are labeled "Race Prejudice, Color Hatred and Autocracy."

Perhaps the best short commentary on what happens is a cartoon by Yardley from the Baltimore *Sun* (FIGURE 140). The true picture of Uncle Sam, holding dove and olive branch, is changed by Red propaganda into a bellicose threat bearing H-bomb and bloody sword. As world opinion watches, the Soviet emissary intones: "We want peace, but warmongering Uncle Sam won't permit it!"

In view of the abuse to which Uncle Sam is often subjected overseas, it has been urged that if we must have a symbol,

117

Figure 139

some less contentious figure should be used, such as Columbia or Miss Liberty.[1] What is overlooked in such suggestions is that political adversaries can and do distort any symbol for their purposes. Even Columbia has on occasion been depicted in unfriendly cartoons as a vinegary old harridan. As Harvard historian Arthur Schlesinger, Jr. points out: "It is not our folk symbols which determine the attitudes of others toward us; it is our performance."[2] And he adds: "Every generation of American life re-creates Uncle Sam in its own image. If Uncle Sam currently strikes others as absurd or hypocritical, we are only escaping from reality if we hold accountable the cartoonist's stereotype rather than ourselves." Crane Brinton, another Harvard history professor, agrees: "The figure of Uncle Sam

is now no more than a symbol . . . into which lover or hater can pour his feelings." He declares that "there is no way to find for a nation a one-way symbol that will always promote nice feelings and always discourage unpleasant ones. More important, Uncle Sam is the kind of symbol that even a very determined pressure group in our culture cannot alter. It would probably take a revolution or a dictator to change him. I, for one, much prefer the old gentleman as he is, with his many good points intact; he is unassuming, clearly has a sense of humor and doesn't look at all like the organization man."[3]

Uncle Sam traces back to the dawning years of the Republic. He is a folk character who was spontaneously evoked out of the needs of the people. In appearance

118

Figure 140

he may be archaic, but he still represents the spirit of sturdy individualism so much prized by Americans — an attribute which has not wholly vanished. One suspects that he will be around for quite a while.[4]

13: Uncle Sam Today

Although Uncle Sam is mainly a cartoon character, his name and fame are reflected elsewhere. He appears at pageants and fairs, and was long a standard fixture of the circus. Dan Rice, one of the first great American clowns, is credited with introducing the Uncle Sam character to the big show shortly after the five Ringling brothers started their circus in 1870.

When a West Berlin vaudeville act represented a race between a Russian tortoise and an American hare a few years ago, the latter was dressed to look like Uncle Sam. And when a U. S. Army pilot flew mercy missions to sick youngsters in Austria, just after World War II, he was known as "Uncle Sam" to thousands. At dozens of pageants, both in the United States and abroad, Uncle Sam appears in person, especially on the Fourth of July.

George M. Cohan wrote and produced many Broadway hits in which Uncle Sam was prominently featured.

It is the cartoonist, however, who gives Uncle Sam his meaning in our daily lives. Rollin Kirby observed in the thirties that among the cartoon symbols

. . . the figure of Uncle Sam is the most overworked of all. Each day he looks sternly out at the world from his place on the editorial page and views with alarm, warns, dictates, with pontifical fervor. Rarely does he laugh, for he is the Federal voice, and as such, deals only in weighty matters. He tells kings, potentates, labor unions, corrupt officeholders, and swindling trusts (depending on whether he is a Republican or Democratic Uncle Sam) where they "get off." In his gayer moments he welcomes transatlantic flyers and channel swimmers and, in his sadder moments, stands with bowed head at the death of a public man of importance. He is ubiquitous, untiring, and a good deal of a bore. Yet the management of a daily cartoon would be difficult without his valuable services.[1]

If the cartoonist is Uncle Sam's keeper, expositor, and delineator, his responsibilities are quite as awesome as those of the official who writes his name on a treaty next to the Great Seal of the United States. This raises the question: what kind of people *are* the cartoonists? As a group, are they equipped to express and explain Uncle Sam to peoples both in this country and abroad?

In the hands of a master, the cartoon can rise to the stature of great art. Indeed, the word cartoon derives from the sketches which the artists of the Renaissance drew, to be worked up later as paintings. The cartoon can suggest much more than it actually shows. But the cartoonist labors under the necessity of never overshooting the understanding of his mass audience. Sometimes he feels constrained thereby to speak only in clichés and truisms. Often he works under editorial direction and repression. This is why it is usually the fortunate free spirit who produces the best examples of the cartoonist's art. The great cartoonist must fight for his independence. Nast had to defend his principles many times. When David Low agreed to work for Lord Beaverbrook's London *Evening Standard,* he inserted a proviso in his contract allowing him complete freedom of expression, whether or not it conflicted with the editorial policy of the paper. Despite the letters of alarm from Disgusted and Constant Reader, Beaverbrook supported Low throughout their long association, a relationship unusual in journalistic history.

In his autobiography, Low tells how, not content with long-range inspection of the changing scene, he went about meeting and analyzing the leading figures of his time, and getting their views from their own lips. He studied the masters of his craft: Gillray, Rowlandson, Leech, Tenniel, Partridge. He was as much concerned with the proper execution of the idea as with the idea itself. When his pains went unappreciated save. by those who saw only their own prejudices flattered, he began to wonder.

Was that why I sat up half the night fretting to get the right simper, frown or smirk on Baldwin's face? Was that the average response to the exercise of mind and imagination involved in. playing with line values as a musician plays with notes on the piano, to produce effects of farce, fantasy or tragedy? Was that why I strained my ingenuity inventing ways of drawing things that are undrawable, like the invisible man, say, or a couple of isosceles triangles having a fight, or a man chasing a dog on the blind side of a wall? Or why I strove to express emotions in familiar visual terms, to create — create was the word — pictorial symbols for ideas that have no shape or substance, like Freedom, War, Peace, Labour, Slump, Prosperity, Europe, Britain, and so on?[2]

Low believes that caricature is the greatest of the arts, because it involves to a surpassing degree the essentials of selection and emphasis. It is true that the cartoonist must be a great deal more than a gag man. His work usually appears on either the front page or among the editorials. It is often the first thing the reader sees. This is a place of responsibility and power, and those who fill it should be properly prepared for their jobs. Most of them, however, are self-educated. Many cartoonists possess the kind of bright, inquiring minds found so often in the newspaper business — more than a trace disillusioned, but keenly interested in the world panorama for all that. Considering the significance of their work, too little has been offered by either schools of art or journalism to educate them for their jobs. Some of the best have come from the field of sports cartooning, which has also produced some of the top columnists. It may be that no amount of instruction can produce a Nast or a Low. They must be born with a certain inner drive which impels them irresistibly toward the graphic depiction of ideas.

These are the men who give us daily their scores of varied interpretations of Uncle Sam and his doings. A quick glance at one day's production of Uncle Sams in the nation's press shows how varied are their techniques and their conceptions. It is remarkable that, although Uncle Sam is shown in so many shapes and sizes, and with such varying degrees of emphasis, his total personality is not thereby adulterated or altered.

If one were to seek for faults in the current crop of Uncle Sams, they would be found chiefly in the failure to develop all the rich potential of his character. Considering the enormous appeal of Will Rogers to the American people, especially when he discoursed on political themes, why have so few cartoonists sought to endow our Uncle with some of Rogers' distinctively American warmth and drollery? One recognizes that Uncle Sam represents the Federal power, and as such has a certain dignity to maintain. However, our best-loved leaders have always been those who took their jobs seriously, but not themselves. Perhaps the best Uncle Sams are still to be drawn.

Meanwhile Uncle Sam references are multiplying rather than decreasing. This is probably because of the constantly larger part the national government plays in our lives. Inspection of the newspapers and magazines of fifty years ago reveals how comparatively seldom the headline and editorial writers used the term. Today, with government reaching into so many new areas, there is often no better or faster way to indicate that a course of action is being considered in Washington, or has been determined there, than to say Uncle Sam did it.

In his modern role as world benefactor, Uncle Sam was paired with Santa Claus in a cartoon by Dorman H. Smith for NEA Service (FIGURE 141). Santa says: "Thanks, Sam, with your help I'm a huge success!"

Paradoxically, there are almost no mentions of Uncle Sam in the official publications that come from the Government Printing Office. Whether this is because bureaucrats do not identify themselves with Uncle, or because they are afraid that he is too popular with all persons and parties to be safely political, is not clear. But in Washington itself, where Uncle Sam may be presumed to walk abroad both at noonday and nightfall, and to exercise at all times the fullness of his authority, visual and verbal notice of his presence is perhaps rarest. No one has ever seen him at the White House, or in the halls of Congress. He has no offices, nor does the Bureau of the Budget ever consider estimates for his maintenance. In political campaigns, orators would no more think of calling upon him to witness their records than British candidates would call upon John Bull or the reigning monarch. Even so, it would appear that the average politico has more than a little respect for Uncle Sam. And this illustrates the curious ambivalence of his personality. As the ancient and perpetual emblem of the U. S. Government, Uncle Sam has come to represent, to the officeholders themselves, a higher authority of which they themselves are servants — the will of the people. For in America the final power is vested in the individual citizen. This is our ruling principle, and Uncle Sam, being a staunch and stalwart old individualist, well exemplifies it. That may in part explain the strength of his firm and continuing hold on the public imagination.

No robot, no collectivist mass man in boots and tunic is Uncle Sam. He is as he has always been, a disciple of liberty under law, convinced that every man is a little different from every other man, and entitled to whatever eccentricities he may wish to cultivate. Uncle Sam is above all a human being. Freedom is his philosophy, and all the wordy dialecticians of the left and right will never sway him from this, the central core of his being.

Figure 141

In today's struggle for the world between those who cherish human rights and those dedicated to statism, Uncle Sam simply extends to a larger sphere what he has stood for in America all along. As the living symbol of individual freedom, he demonstrates an adaptability and a fertility of resource which augur well for him and for his principles as America heads into the space age. The way may be hard and long, but he has been in plenty of desperate corners before. He was born in one, and ever since, the bigger the challenge he has met, the greater his achievement in eventually winning through.

123

References

Chapter 1

1. One of the best authorities in this field is Harold Bayley, *The Lost Language of Symbolism*, 2 Vols. (New York, Barnes & Noble, 1912; reprinted 1951).

Chapter 2

1. Letter to Bradford's *Pennsylvania Journal* (December 27, 1775).
2. John Adams, *Familiar Letters of John Adams and His Wife Abigail Adams, during the Revolution*, Charles Francis Adams, ed. (New York, Hurd & Houghton, 1876), p. 210.
3. For background, see Howard Payson Arnold, *Historic Sidelights* (New York, Harper, 1899). A delightfully discursive work that takes many casual tangents.
4. *Works of Thomas Jefferson*, Paul Leicester Ford, ed., 10 Vols. (New York, Putnam, 1892-99), Vol. 1, p. 420.
5. *Audacibus annuit coeptis* (favor my daring undertaking) is from the *Aeneid*, Book 9, Verse 625 (also in the *Georgics*, Vol. 1, p. 40). *Magnus ab integro seclorum nascitur ordo* (the great series of ages begins anew) is from the fourth eclogue, fifth verse.
6. In his "Remarks and Explanation," Charles Thomson wrote: "The Escutcheon is composed of the chief & pale, the two most honorable ordinaries. The pieces, paly, represent the Several States all joined in one solid compact entire, supporting a Chief, which unites the whole & represents Congress. The Motto alludes to this union. The pales in the arms are kept closely united by the chief and the chief depends on that Union & the strength resulting from it for its support, to denote the Confederacy of the United States of America & the preservation of their Union through Congress. The colours of the pales are those used in the flag of the United States of America; White signifies purity and innocence, Red, hardiness & valour, and Blue, the colour of the Chief, signifies vigilance, perseverance & justice. The Olive branch and arrows denote the power of peace & war which is exclusively vested in Congress. The Constellation denotes a new

State taking its place and rank among other sovereign powers. The Escutcheon is born on the breast of an American Eagle without any other supporters, to denote that the United States of America ought to rely on their own Virtue.

"Reverse. The pyramid signifies Strength and Duration: the Eye over it & the Motto allude to the many signal interpositions of providence in favour of the American cause. The date underneath is that of the Declaration of Independence and the words under it signify the beginning of the new America Æra, which commences from that date." See *The History of the Seal of the United States* (U. S. Department of State, Washington, 1909), p. 42.

7. However, *The Seal of the United States,* published by the Department of State in 1957, comments as follows on the act of 1884 in which Congress authorized new cuttings of both obverse and reverse: "Although the statement has frequently been made that no die of the reverse was cut at that time — that that part of the act was left unexecuted — evidence has recently been found indicating that such a die may then in fact have been cut — though never put to use."

8. Franklin wrote to his daughter on January 26, 1784, apropos of the eagle on the badge of the Order of the Society of the Cincinnati, which some objected to because it looked like a turkey:

"For my part I wish that the bald eagle had not been chosen as the representative of our country; he is a bird of bad moral character; he does not get his living honestly; you may have seen him perched on some dead tree, where, too lazy to fish for himself, he watches the labor of the fishing-hawk; and when that diligent bird has at length taken a fish, and is bearing it to his nest for the support of his mate and young ones, the bald eagle pursues him, and takes it from him. With all this injustice he is never in good case; but like those among men who live by sharping and robbing, he is generally poor, and often very lousy. Besides, he is a rank coward; the little *kingbird,* not bigger than a sparrow, attacks him boldly and drives him out of the district. He is therefore by no means a proper emblem for the brave and honest Cincinnati of America, who have driven all the *kingbirds* from our country; though exactly fit for that order of knights, which the French call *Chevaliers d'Industrie.*

"I am, on this account, not displeased that the figure is not known as a bald eagle, but looks more like a turkey. For in truth, the turkey is in comparison a much more respectable bird, and withal a true original native of America. Eagles have been found in all countries, but the turkey was peculiar to ours; the first of the species seen in Europe, being brought to France by the Jesuits from Canada, and served up at the wedding table of Charles the Ninth. He is, besides (though a little vain and silly, it is true, but not the worse emblem for that), a bird of courage, and would not hesitate to attack a grenadier of the British guards, who should presume to invade his farmyard with a *red* coat on." See *Works of Franklin,* John Bigelow, ed. (New York, Putnam, 1887-88), Vol. III, p. 252.

9. While this is usually attributed to Secretary Chase, it should be pointed out that a phrase almost like it occurs in the third stanza of Francis Scott Key's "Defence of Fort McHenry" which became "The Star Spangled Banner."

Then conquer we must, when our cause it is just,
And this be our motto, — "In God is our trust;"

Key, a lawyer of Georgetown, Washington, D. C., left Baltimore under a flag of truce on September 3, 1814, to effect the release of a friend "Old Dr. (William) Beanes, of Marlborough," who had been captured by the British. . . . In preparation for landings, the British bombarded the fort the night of September 13-14. Anxiously Key paced the deck through the dark hours, following the hissing arc of each shell and wondering what dawn would reveal. At the first light he saw the American flag still flying. The attack had failed. Such was his emotion that he jotted down on the back of a letter several lines which had

126

come to him during his vigil. He finished the poem on the way back to Baltimore. First published as a handbill, titled "The Bombardment of Fort McHenry," it won immediate popularity and was printed in the *Baltimore American* on September 21, 1814, with "Bombardment" changed to "Defence." Key himself had suggested that the lines be set to an old English tune, "Anacreon in Heaven." . . . The flag about which the song was written was made to order by the widow Mary Pickersgill, who lived nearby. It still exists, much tattered and torn, in the National Museum in Washington. . . . It should be of interest that this old Star-Spangled Banner underwent the baptism of fire that gave birth to the national anthem, on September 13, 1814, which was Uncle Sam's birthday! See George Henry Preble, Rear-Admiral, U.S.N., *Origin and History of the American Flag* (Philadelphia, Nicholas L. Brown, 1917).

It should also be noted that the motto of an early crest of the state of Rhode Island was "In God We Hope."

10. Yankee Doodle is a musical gypsy known in and reported from many nations. One tradition is that the original song was written about Oliver Cromwell, and was called "Nankee Doodle." The earliest printed version of words for the tune is in *Walsh's Collection of Dances for the Year 1750*. There it is in six–eight time and is entitled "Fisher's Jig." To this were sung the words of the nursery rhyme:

> Lucy Locket lost her pocket;
> Kitty Fisher found it;
> Not a bit of money in it,
> Only binding round it.

Both ladies were well-known in the gay circles around Charles II. See Preble, *op. cit.*

In 1750 Henry Fielding wrote a satire, "Tom Thumb the Great," with three characters named Doodle, Noodle, and Foodle. Thus "Doodle" was current as a name of ridicule, and it was easy to put "Yankee" in front of it and in two words express one's opinion of the colonial type.

Albert Matthews, *Uncle Sam, History of the Term* (Worcester, Massachusetts, American Antiquarian Society Proceedings, 1908), new series, Vol. 19, pp. 21-65, quotes the *New York Journal* of October 13, 1768, as reporting that when the British troops arrived at Boston in 1768, it was stated, on September 29, that "the Yankey Doodle Song was the Capital Piece in their Band of Music." Evidently with the purpose of annoying the good people of Boston, the British persisted in playing the air at intervals for another seven years. Matthews says that the air of Yankee Doodle made its first appearance under that name in Act I, Scene 3 of Andrew Barton's "The Disappointment; Or, The Force of Credulity: A New American Comic Opera," first printed in Philadelphia in 1767. The copy in the Ridgway Branch, Library Company of Philadelphia, is inscribed in ink on the title page: "by Col. Thomas Forest of Germantown. S." Bartlett reports that "the song is said to be identical with one sung by the agricultural laborers in the Netherlands. Kossuth and his fellow Hungarians, while in this country, are said to have recognized it as one of the old national airs of their native land. And recently Buckingham Smith, our then Secretary of Legation at Madrid, asserted that it is the ancient 'Sword Dance of the Biscayans.' "

See John Russell Bartlett, *Dictionary of Americanisms*. (Boston, Little, Brown, 1859.)

In the Dutch version, it was sung at harvest time:

> "Yanker didel, doodel down,
> Didel, dudel lauter,
> Yanke viver, voover vown,
> Botermith und Yauther."

See Preble, *op. cit.*

According to Matthews, the "Father and I" version was not written until 1775, and therefore could not have been the "original." The words usually sung are supposed to have been written by "a gentleman of Connecticut, a short time after Gen. Washington's last visit to New England." He says that the words made their earliest known appearance in print in 1790, having been written into Royall Tyler's play "The Contrast," first acted in 1789. [An excerpt appears in Chapter 3.] Earlier printed versions may well have been circulated, but if so they were ephemeral. The song itself, whatever its origins, had and still has the living quality of true folk music. And this despite — or perhaps because of — its early significance. As late as 1785, Grose's *Classical Dictionary of the Vulgar Tongue,* published in London, defined "Yankey, or Yankey Doodle" as "a booby or country lout, a name given to New England men in North America."

11. Bartlett, *op. cit.*
12. Allen Johnson, *Jefferson and His Colleagues,* in "Chronicles of America" series (New Haven, Yale University Press, 1921), Vol. 15, p. 262.

CHAPTER 3

1. Bartlett, *op. cit.*
2. Constance Rourke gives an excellent evocation of the Yankee spirit. She reports that about 1825, Yankee plays began to appear on American stages all over the country. In each the Yankee was the looming figure. The contrast was usually drawn between the honest, plain American and the "silly, foppish, infamous Englishman." The Yankee "might be a peddler, a sailor, a Vermont wool-dealer, or merely a Green Mountain boy who traded and drawled and upset calculations; he was Lot Sapsago or Jedidiah Homebred or Jerusalem Dutiful; sometimes he was a sailor. But always he was the symbolic American. Unless he appeared as a tar his costume hardly varied: he wore a white bell-crowned hat, a coat with long tails that was usually blue, eccentric red trousers, and long boot-straps. Brother Jonathan had in fact turned into Uncle Sam. Half bravado, half cockalorum, this Yankee revealed traits considered deplorable by British travelers; he was indefatigably rural, sharp, uncouth, witty. Here were the manners of the Americans! Peddling,

swapping, practical joking, might have been national preoccupations. He burst periodically into song, with variations of 'Yankee Doodle,' with local ballads celebrating Yankee exploits, or chanteys. Some of the plays verged upon the operatic, and the prevailing high national pitch was repeated by casual allusions. A tavern was called 'The Sign of the Spread Eagle.' Beneath this aegis roamed the Briton, still wicked, still mannered and over-polished, either rich or nefariously seeking riches, and always defeated by simple rural folk to the accompaniment of loud laughter. . . ." See Constance Rourke, *American Humor, A Study of the National Character* (New York, Harcourt, 1931).

3. Albert Matthews, *Brother Jonathan* (Cambridge, Wilson & Son, 1902). Reprinted from *Transactions, Colonial Society of Massachusetts, 1900-02,* Vol. VII, pp. 94-122.
4. The people saluted those who, it seemed to them, best mirrored the Yankee character. No one, probably, contributed more to this image than George Handel Hill. He was a happy-go-lucky type who made the nuances of Yankee portraiture his own. He wrote and delivered many Yankee sketches. "His Yankees were quiet and low-voiced. They whittled a great deal and talked quite as much, but never very loud. They might have been evolved over hasty pudding and cider, at quilting bees or husking parties. . . . His lecture called 'A Learned Society' was a small comic monument to the New England thirst for abstruse discussion. He was full of simple satire, and gave many a sly thrust at New England pride before his native audiences, even touching on the character of the original Pilgrims, whom he appeared to regard with bored irreverence.

"Yankee speech with its slow-running rhythms and high pitch — as if an inner voice were speaking below the audible one — was well adapted to the monologue. Its sound was subtly varied; the cautious drawl served to feel a way among the listeners. As Lowell pointed out some years later, Yankee speech was not so much a dialect as a lingo; that is,

128

its oddities were consciously assumed. It was another form of masquerade. Homely comparisons belonged to it — 'strong as whitleather,' 'so thin you could pitch him clear *through* a flute.' Hill used these sparely: 'If you catch me there again, you'll catch a white weasel asleep, *I* tell you.' . . . For the mock lectures as for the plays Hill continued to wear the flaxen wig, the red-white-and-blue costume, the high boot-straps and tall white hat of the nationalistic Yankee." See Rourke, *op. cit.*

5. Quoted in *Rebellion Record, 1861–1865*, Frank Moore, ed. (New York, Van Nostrand, 1867), Vol. IV, p. 69.

CHAPTER 4

1. Matthews, *op. cit.*
2. "The Trojan Greens, a rifle company, wore green coats with facings, collars, and cuffs of black material trimmed with gold lacing. The band on the hat was green. They carried tomahawks instead of bayonets. The Troy Fusileers, a light infantry company, had blue coats with red facings, collars, and cuffs. Their hats were similar to those of the Trojan Greens, with red bands. The Troy Invincibles, also a light infantry company, were outfitted like the Fusileers, but the shako had a visor with a brass shield, white knotted cord trimming looped around the front and rear. The drawing shows the three outfits in summer uniforms. Their pants were made of white canvas material." Letter to the author June 22, 1959 from John J. Demers, Troy, New York, member of the Company of Military Collectors and Historians of Washington, D. C.; Assistant to Col. Frederick P. Todd, Director of the Military Museum at West Point.
3. John Woodworth, *Reminiscences of Troy from Its Settlement in 1790 to 1807* (Albany, J. Munsell, 1860).
4. Arthur Weise, *History of the City of Troy* (Troy, William H. Young, 1876).

CHAPTER 5

1. In the General Abstract of Provisions as supplied by Elbert Anderson, Jr., under the terms of his contract dated 7th November 1811, and letter from the Secretary of War of 25th February, 1812, appear several shipments from Samuel Wilson. One item notes nine barrels of pork and 251 of beef; another 17 casks of whiskey from Wilson, Mann & Co.; another 462 bushels of salt for pickling, hooping and overhauling 1,733½ barrels of pork and 1,570 barrels of beef stored at Troy. For the meat the contractor was paid $2,340.80, and for the salt, $617.62. These quantities were small compared with those packed for the same contractor by Samuel's brother Nathaniel, then operating in Albany, who supplied 1,921 barrels of pork and 129 barrels of beef. It is possible that the two had already established the working agreement, which in 1817 took both to Catskill, where they jointly established and ran another packing yard. From the National Archives, Records of the Office of the Adjutant General, Record group No. 94.
2. Commodore Rodgers' name is misspelled in the broadside as "Rogers."
3. This notion of Uncle Sam's bounty was expressed in the postwar years by a song which was in key with the westward migration.

Of all the mighty nations
In the east or in the west,
O this glorious Yankee nation
Is the greatest and the best.
We have room for all creation
And our banner is unfurled,
Here's a general invitation
To the people of the world.

Come from every nation,
Come from every way,
Our lands, they are broad enough;
Don't be alarmed,
For Uncle Sam is rich enough
To give us all a farm.

These lines were written and sung by Jesse Hutchinson, Jr., of Milford, New Hampshire, and his Hutchinson Family Singers.
4. Thus far, no authenticated likeness of Samuel Wilson has been found. In 1936 WPA researchers sought in vain for a

picture to be used in the *American Guide.* There is a tantalizing reference to portraits of both Uncle Sam and Aunt Betsey in a letter which appeared that year in the *Troy Record.* In it Mrs. Clara Wilson Hicks states that as a young girl she saw them both at Albert Wilson's home. But no amount of looking has ever turned up the missing portraits. Perhaps they are now serving as decorative pieces in the home of someone who does not even know what treasures he possesses.

5. *New York Times,* March 19, 1899.

CHAPTER 6

1. Some confusion has been occasioned by the fact that Edward Wilson's family Bible noted the birth date of his son Samuel as Sept. 16, 1766, a fact reported by Lucius Wilson in his 1917 account. However, this date was set down from memory many years later. Much more reliable are the records of Arlington, Massachusetts, the birthplace, in which, according to James J. Golden, Town Clerk, it is recorded that Samuel Wilson was born on Sept. 13, 1766. Arlington, Massachusetts, Vital Records to 1850, published in 1904, p. 47, quoted in letter to the author October 17, 1958 from Mr. Golden.

2. Lucius Wilson wrote in 1917 that his great-great-grandfather Wilson was one of three brothers who emigrated from Scotland "some time previous to the Revolution." One settled in Medford, Mass., and his son, Edward, was Samuel Wilson's father. Of the other two brothers, one settled in Connecticut and the other went into the state of New York, "but of him nothing definite was ever learned."

3. However, Mr. Warren Edward Russell believes that the Wilson property extended "from what is now Water Street approximately to Railroad Avenue, along Massachusetts Avenue and back to near Mill Brook." He feels that the Wilson residence was more to the west of the railroad station. Letter to the author June 7, 1959 from Mr. Russell.

4. Frederick Mackenzie, *A British Fusilier in Revolutionary Boston* (Cambridge, Harvard University Press, 1930).

5. Hannah Winthrop to Mercy Warren (April or May, 1775), Massachusetts Historical Society, Warren-Adams Letters, Vol. II, p. 410.

6. The story that Samuel Wilson acted as a "service boy" during the Revolution has been widely reprinted ever since it was published in the *Troy Times-Record* on July 3, 1936, in an article by William Bartlett. Mr. Bartlett asserted that Sam enlisted on March 2, 1781 at Conway, New Hampshire, at the age of fifteen years, and that it was necessary for his father to give a bond for him because of his youth. The principal duty of a service boy was to guard and care for the cattle intended as food for the troops. The story is a beguiling one because it gives Sam an active part in the Revolution, and also because it explains his entry later into the meat-packing business. However, it appears to be wholly without foundation. Research by Miss Elizabeth Orton Jones has proved the Samuel Wilson in question to have been another person entirely. He was a life-long resident of Conway, New Hampshire, and the records show that he was a well-known citizen of that town. Moreover, Conway was a good hundred miles north of Mason, and it is not likely that Samuel *and* his father would have walked or ridden so far. Finally, Miss Charlotte D. Conover, librarian of the New Hampshire Historical Society, said (in a letter of July 2, 1956) ". . . we cannot substantiate any Revolutionary service for Samuel Wilson who lived in Mason, New Hampshire. In the official Revolutionary records for New Hampshire, several by that name are listed from various towns, but we cannot from the records identify the 'original of Uncle Sam.' "

7. It has been generally assumed that Samuel Wilson must have learned brick-making while he lived in Mason. This assumption is strengthened by the fact that there were clay banks on the farms of two residents of Brookline, New Hampshire, only two miles east of Ma-

son, where bricks were being made as early as 1780. Many of the houses in Mason were built of these bricks. Since this was the only focus of brickmaking activity in the area, it must have been there that Samuel and Ebenezer Wilson picked up the knowledge which they put to such good use in Troy immediately after their arrival. Letter to the author from Miss Elizabeth Orton Jones, Mason, New Hampshire, October 29, 1956.

8. Article "Uncle Sam" by Miss Jessie F. Wheeler, for many years reference librarian at the Troy Public Library, in *Troy Record*, February 16, 1920.

9. François Alexandre Frédéric, duc de La Rochefoucauld Liancourt, *Travels through the United States of North America,* 2 Vols. (London, R. Phillips, 1799).

10. His grandson recalled that although the Reverend Ebenezer Hill was a small man physically, he made a deep impression on the life of his community. In *Ebenezer Hill, the Little Minister of Mason, New Hampshire,* published in New York in 1923, Charles Ebenezer Hill said that his grandfather was "barely five feet in stature, but of perfect proportions, with delicate, clean-shaven features, firm lips, quick eyes — neat, sprightly, genial." He also gives us a good picture of Mason as it was shortly after the Wilsons moved there. "In 1790 there were about a hundred and ten houses scattered over the town, the most of them miserably poor. Only one house had any paint, and only three rooms in the town were papered. There was not a wheel carriage or a single sleigh. Whole families came to church on an oxcart or sled. Travel was generally on foot or horseback. It was the day of the pillion, 'a comfortable and commodious seat,' says our Minister, and it was no strange thing to see a single horse carrying on his back a man and woman and one or two small children. The Minister on his candidating journeys probably rode on horseback, with a fair supply of spotless linen and Calvinistic sermons in his saddlebags." The Reverend Hill had a propensity for begetting twins.

He had three wives, all of whom he married within a ten-year span, and he fathered fourteen children in all. The large family was fond of music and delighted in "performing anthems," in which the Wilsons and other neighbors probably joined. About 1822 he "banished from his cupboard the square case-bottle of Medford rum, from which he had so often drawn cheer and comfort." He also gave up chewing tobacco. It is a curious coincidence that the Reverend Hill was born in 1766, the same year as Samuel Wilson, and died the same year — 1854.

11. Some accounts mention a fifth child, Sally, who died in infancy. Of the Wilson offspring, only Benjamin and Albert survived to adulthood. Albert had no children. Benjamin Wilson practiced law in Troy and New York City. He married Mary Wood at Auburn, New York, in 1839 while she was attending the Emma Willard Female Seminary at Troy. They had four children, Sarah W., born in August, 1841, died May 1, 1855; Elizabeth, who died in infancy; Emma B., born in New York City in 1844, died in 1916 at seventy-two years of age, unmarried; and Marion, born November 4, 1849. Mary Wood Wilson died at Syracuse in 1869. Marion Wilson was ten years old when her father died. Thereafter she moved to Syracuse with her mother and sister, and after her mother died, to Minnesota. She was married in 1876 to Frederick C. Sheldon at Fairbault, Minnesota. They lived most of their married life in Kansas City, Missouri. Mr. Sheldon died in 1929. They had two sons, Carlton Wood Sheldon, born in 1880, and Harry, born in 1882, who died the same year. Carlton Wood Sheldon married Lilly Parkes, and they had a daughter, Helen Marion, who married Robert Brockett. The Brocketts had a daughter, Betty Sheldon, born in 1930. Betty Brockett married William Joseph Hambuchen of Conway, Arkansas. They have two children, Helen and Robert Hambuchen, who are the youngest offspring of Uncle Sam in the direct line of descent.

12. James D. Pinckney, *Reminiscences of*

Catskill (Catskill, New York, J. B. Hall, 1868), p. 51.

13. This was incorrect. The story appeared in the *Troy Northern Budget*, May 21, 1830. Ebenezer Wilson had died in 1825.

14. In 1929 the *Troy Record* reported that Uncle Sam's niece, Mrs. Jennie Gross, was still living in Lansingburgh. Mrs. Gross was the daughter of Benjamin Mann, whose sister Betsey was the wife of Samuel Wilson. Mrs. Gross remembered how as a little girl she went to her Aunt Betsey's home on Ferry Street, and watched her aunt, then nearly a hundred years old, cut out bookmarks from colored paper. She said that the wife of Uncle Sam was a character known throughout the city, and was as popular with the people, especially the young ones, as her husband. Her mind was clear, although as she approached the century mark she was compelled to remain in her bed. See the *Troy Record*, February 19, 1929.

15. Apparently Samuel Wilson was a Baptist in his earlier years. Records of the old Third Street Baptist Church testify to that fact. Bricks for this church were provided by E. and S. Wilson at a cost of $457.31. Samuel Wilson was elected a trustee of the church in 1808. He was present at meetings, as shown by the records, until 1816. He lived in Catskill from 1817 to 1822, and during that period he is believed to have attended the First Baptist Church there, along with his brother Nathaniel.

16. This is what Josiah Webber recalled about Lucy Wilson when, at the age of eighty, he wrote his reminiscences. "The day I was fifteen I went to live with Captain Thomas Wilson. I worked about the house in the morning, then with the men in the field. Mr. Wilson's mother couldn't walk but after being dressed would sit in a wheel chair; she smoked a pipe and I would light it for her. There were no matches in those days, so I had to put in a coal of fire and take a few whiffs, and hand it to her. I was a great favorite with her. She was quite aged. That summer her son Samuel came to see her and his brother's family. He was the man that furnished supplies for the United States Army; the packages were marked U.S. Some of the employees asked what it meant. Someone replied 'Uncle Sam.' The States have been known by that name ever since. . . . [He] brought some things to his mother such as oranges and fine-cut tobacco."

This account is from a copy of a manuscript in the possession of Miss Elizabeth Orton Jones, entitled, "Incidents in the Life of Josiah Webber of Mason, New Hampshire." It was dictated by Josiah Webber to his daughter, Genevieve Webber Hastings, who wrote it down sometime during the 1890's.

Josiah Webber was born in 1815; therefore this incident would have occurred about 1830. At that time Lucy Wilson was a little over ninety-one years of age. Sally Wilson, daughter of Capt. Thomas, was born in 1805.

Miss Jones says: "It is evident from this that by 1830 Samuel Wilson was quite a notable and fairly affluent gentleman and that the legend was well established about him."

CHAPTER 8

1. However, Britons who visited the United States sometimes used the term as the Americans did. In fact, the first mention of Uncle Sam by a foreign writer is found in an account of travels through the United States, published in 1823, by William Faux, a British farmer. His trip was "principally undertaken to ascertain by positive evidence, the condition and probable prospects of British emigrants." In his book he refers to *"Uncle Sam's* western mail," "one of *Uncle Sam's* high sheriffs," "Harper's Ferry — *Uncle Sam's* grand central depot of arms and ammunition," "the metropolis of *Uncle Sam*," and "the state seminary . . . built by *Uncle Sam*." He concluded that *"Uncle Sam* is a right slick, mighty fine, smart, big man." See William Faux, *Memorable Days in America* (London, W. Simpkin and R. Marshall, 1823), pp. 126, 140, 162, 188, 215.

2. Frank Weitenkampf comments on how

the stars have wandered about on Uncle Sam's costume, "settling at various times on shirt (*Harper's Weekly,* Aug. 10, 1861, and Dec. 13, 1862), shirt collar, (Nast in *Harper's Weekly,* Nov. 9 and 16, 1872; Keppler in *Leslie's,* Jan. 23, 1875), vest, (H. L. Stephens in *Vanity Fair,* June 28, 1862, John McLenan in *Harper's Weekly,* Aug. 23, 1862, and Keppler in *Leslie's,* March 13, 1875 and in *Puck* July 30, 1879, Aug. 25, 1880, May 2, 1883, Aug. 22, 1888), trousers, (*Harper's Weekly,* Dec. 13, 1862), nightcap, (*Harper's Weekly,* Dec. 21, 1861), hat, (W. H. Walker, 1899). . . ." He adds that later on the stars were generally placed on the coat. See Frank Weitenkampf, *Uncle Sam Through the Years, A Cartoon Record.* (New York, Typescripts at New York Historical Society, and New York Public Library, 1949.)

However, the most acceptable modern version seems to be stars on the hatband only, though some cartoonists continue to sprinkle a few on the vest and coat cuffs. As for the stripes, they have adorned the trousers almost from the beginning, and occasionally the shirt. In recent years they have also become the usual decoration of the hat, above the band of stars.

CHAPTER 10

1. Albert Bigelow Paine, *Thomas Nast, His Period and His Pictures* (New York, Macmillan, 1904).

CHAPTER 11

1. Weitenkampf *(op. cit.)* says that "one of [Matt] Morgan's cartoons had Uncle posing as Oberon *(Leslie's,* Jan. 24, 1874), which recalls the many roles that he was made to play by cartoonists, with natural changes in costume. He has appeared as Hamlet (Nast, *Harper's Weekly,* 1876), a barkeep *(Lantern,* 1852), Samson, *(Vanity Fair,* Jan. 25, 1862), Santa Claus, *(Leslie's,* Jan. 2, 1875), a policeman, (Keppler in *Les-*

lie's, Dec. 26, 1874), and as Sam Quixote, (about 1874, probably in *Leslie's),* with armor over his costume. The last is one of the few cases when he is shown on horseback. . . ." Weitenkampf also notes that at various times *Puck* showed Uncle as Moses, Wotan, Hercules, a jailer, barber, ringmaster, judge, farmer, and in other roles to suit the situation.

CHAPTER 12

1. Allan Nevins, "Let's Disown Uncle Sam," *New York Times Magazine,* March 1, 1959.
2. "Is Uncle Sam Obsolete? — A Fiery Debate," *New York Times Magazine,* April 12, 1959.
3. *Ibid.*
4. Many other attempts have been made to alter Uncle Sam or do away with him entirely. In 1937 Professor Clyde R. Miller, of Teachers College, Columbia University, attacked the "penny-pinching, budget-examining, church deacon type" of Uncle Sam. He declared that it was up to the cartoonists and illustrators to come to the rescue with a character displaying the "humor, sense of fun and laughing wit" of the real American. On March 20, 1937, the New York *World-Telegram* ran the opinions of some eminent cartoonists on Professor Miller's suggestion.

Art Young was quoted as doubting that there was any real merit in an Uncle Sam known for "laughing wit." He said that "the figure of Uncle Sam, like the Constitution, has had to submit to amendments. Cartoonists have taken the pictorial right to trim his whiskers, to put trousers on him that are not quite as striped as they used to be, and a coat not wholly covered with stars. They have tried to simplify his dress a little without violating the original concept. Having undergone these slight changes, let us not transfer him into a gay, laughing uncle."

Willard Mullin had his own version: "Easy going, tolerant, a bit of a sport, a quick guy with a dollar, always buying a bridge or a dam on the installment plan, maybe not too solvent, but still our Uncle Sam."

Syd Hoff showed Uncle Sam wearing a nightshirt and carrying a lantern. He explained that this was "the modern Uncle Sam looking for a way out — of what, I don't know."

CHAPTER 13

1. Warren Cox, Rollin Kirby, and Art Young, "Cartoons," *Encyclopedia Britannica*, 14th ed., Vol. IV, p. 950.
2. David Low, *Low's Autobiography* (New York, Simon & Schuster, 1957), p. 155.

Bibliography

ADAMS, JAMES TRUSLOW, *The March of Democracy*. New York, Scribner, 1933, 2 Vols.

ADAMS, JOHN, *Familiar Letters of John Adams and His Wife Abigail Adams, during the Revolution,* Charles Francis Adams, ed. New York, Hurd & Houghton, 1876.

American Caricatures Pertaining to the Civil War. New York, Brentano's, 1918.

AMPHLETT, JAMES, *The Newspaper Press.* London, Whittaker, 1860.

Arlington, Mass., *Vital Records to the Year 1850.* New England Historic Genealogical Society, 1904.

ARNOLD, HOWARD PAYSON, *Historic Sidelights.* New York, Harper, 1899.

BARTLETT, JOHN RUSSELL, *Dictionary of Americanisms.* Boston, Little, Brown, 1859.

BAYLEY, HAROLD, *The Lost Language of Symbolism.* New York, Barnes & Noble, 1912, reprinted 1951, 2 Vols.

BLOCK, HERBERT, *The Herblock Book.* Boston, Beacon Press, 1952.

BOWEN, CATHERINE DRINKER, *John Adams and the American Revolution.* Boston, Little, Brown, 1950.

BRADLEY, LUTHER D., *Cartoons by Bradley.* Chicago, Rand, 1917.

BUCKINGHAM, JOSEPH T., *Specimens of Newspaper Literature.* Boston, Charles C. Little and James Brown, 1850, 2 Vols.

BUTTERFIELD, ROGER, *The American Past.* New York, Simon & Schuster, 1947.

CARMER, CARL, *The Hudson.* New York, Rinehart, 1939.

Complete Works of Benjamin Franklin, The, John Bigelow, ed., New York, Putnam, 1887-88, 10 Vols.

CROSBY, PERCY, *Always Belittlin'.* McLean, Va., privately published, 1933.

CUTTER, BENJAMIN, and WILLIAM R., *History of the Town of Arlington, Massachusetts.* Boston, Clapp & Son, 1880.

CUTTER, WILLIAM R., *Genealogical and Personal Memoirs Relating to the Families of Boston and Eastern Massachusetts.* New York, Lewis Historical Publishing Co., 1910.

D'ALVIELLA, COUNT GOBLET, *The Migration of Symbols.* 1894. Reprinted, New York, University Books, 1956.

DAVENPORT, HOMER C., *Cartoons.* New York, DeWitt Publishing House, 1898.

Diary of the American Revolution, Frank Moore, ed. New York, Scribner, 1860, 2 Vols.

DORSON, RICHARD M., "The Yankee on the Stage." *New England Quarterly*, Vol. 13 (September, 1940), p. 467.

FALKNER, LEONARD, *Forge of Liberty*. New York, Dutton, 1959.

FAUX, WILLIAM, *Memorable Days in America*. London, W. Simpkin and R. Marshall, 1823.

FORBES, ESTHER, *Paul Revere and the World He Lived In*. Boston, Houghton, 1942.

FROST, JOHN, *Book of the Navy*. New York, Appleton, 1842.

HALE, EDWARD EVERETT, *Tarry at Home Travels*. New York, Macmillan, 1906.

HARPER, ROBERT S., *Lincoln and the Press*. New York, McGraw, 1951.

HAYNER, RUTHERFORD, *Troy and Rensselaer County*. New York, Lewis Historical Publishing Co., 1925, 3 Vols.

HILL, CHARLES EBENEZER, *Ebenezer Hill, the Little Minister of Mason, N.H.* New York, T. A. Wright, 1923.

HILL, GEORGE HANDEL, *Yankee story teller's own book; and reciter's pocket companion*. Philadelphia, Turner & Fisher, 1836.

HILL, JOHN BOYNTON, *History of the town of Mason, N.H.* Boston, L. A. Elliott & Co., 1858.

—— *Memoir of Ebenezer Hill, pastor of the Congregational Church in Mason, N.H., 1790 to 1854*. Boston, L. A. Elliott & Co., 1858.

—— *Proceedings of the centennial celebration . . . of the town of Mason, N.H., August 26, 1868*. Boston, Elliott, Thomas & Talbot, 1870.

History of the Seal of the United States. Washington, Department of State, 1909.

HUDSON, FREDERICK, *Journalism in the United States*. New York, Harper, 1873.

HUNT, FREEMAN, *American Anecdotes*, Vol. 2. Boston, Putnam & Hunt, 1830.

Infantry Exercise of the United States Army, abridged for the use of the Militia, 3rd ed. Poughkeepsie, P. Potter, 1819.

JACKSON, MASON, *The Pictorial Press*. London, Hurst & Blackett, 1885.

KIRBY, ROLLIN, *Highlights, A Cartoon History of the Nineteen Twenties*. New York, Payson, 1931.

LA ROCHEFOUCAULD LIANCOURT, FRANCOIS ALEXANDRE FRÉDÉRIC, DUC DE, *Travels through the United States of North America*. London, R. Phillips, 1799, 2 Vols.

LEE, JAMES MELVIN, *History of American Journalism*. New York, Garden City Publishing Co., 1917.

LEHNER, ERNST, *Symbols, Signs and Signets*. Cleveland, World, 1950.

LIPMAN, JEAN, *American Folk Art*. New York, Pantheon, 1948.

LOGEMAN, HENRI, "The Etymology of 'Yankee,'" in *Studies in English Philology* (Minneapolis, 1929), pp. 403-13.

LOSSING, BENSON J., *Pictorial Field-Book of the Revolution*. New York, Harper, 1855, 2 Vols.

—— *Pictorial Field-Book of the War of 1812*. New York, Harper, 1868.

—— *Pictorial History of the Civil War*. Hartford, T. Belknap, 1866.

LOW, DAVID, *Europe Since Versailles*. New York, Penguin Books, 1940.

—— *Low's Autobiography*. New York, Simon & Schuster, 1957.

—— *Years of Wrath, A Cartoon History: 1931–1945*. New York, Simon & Schuster, 1946.

MACKENZIE, FREDERICK, *A British Fusilier in Revolutionary Boston*. Cambridge, Harvard University Press, 1926.

MATTHEWS, ALBERT, *Brother Jonathan*. Cambridge, Wilson & Son, 1902.

—— *The Snake Devices, 1754–1776 and the Constitutional Courant*. Cambridge, Wilson & Son, 1908.

—— "Uncle Sam, History of the Term," in *American Antiquarian Society Proceedings* (Worcester, Massachusetts, 1908), new series, Vol. 19, pp. 21-65.

MONAGHAN, JAY, "Origin of Political Symbols." *Illinois State Historical Society Journal*, Vol. 37 (1944), p. 305.

MURDOCK, HAROLD, *Earl Percy's Dinner Table*. Boston, Houghton, 1907.

—— *The Nineteenth of April, 1775*. Boston, Houghton, 1925.

MURRELL, WILLIAM, *A History of American Graphic Humor, 1747–1865*. New York, Macmillan, for Whitney Museum, 1938, 2 Vols.

NEVINS, ALLAN, and WEITENKAMPF, FRANK, *A Century of Political Cartoons*. New York, Scribner, 1944.

Out of the Crocodile's Mouth, William Nelson, ed. Washington, D. C., Public Affairs Press, 1949.

PAINE, ALBERT BIGELOW, *Thomas Nast, His Period and His Pictures*. New York, Macmillan, 1904.

PARKER, CHARLES S., *Town of Arlington, Past and Present*. Arlington, C. S. Parker & Son, 1907.

Pen is Mightier, The, J. J. Lynx, ed. London, Lindsay Drummond, 1946.

PINCKNEY, JAMES D., *Reminiscences of Catskill*. Catskill, N.Y., J. B. Hall, 1868.

PRATT, FLETCHER, *The Heroic Years — Fourteen Years of the Republic, 1801–1815*. New York, Smith & Haas, 1934.

PRESTON, JOHN HYDE, *Revolution: 1776*. New York, Harcourt, 1933.

Punch Cartoons of the Great War. New York, Doran, 1915.

RAEMAKERS, LOUIS, *Cartoon History of the War*, J. Murray Allison, ed. New York, Century, 1919, 3 Vols.

RAPHAELIAN, H. M., *Signs of Life, A Pictorial Dictionary of Symbols*. New York, Anatol Sivas, 1957.

Rebellion Record. 1861–1865, Frank Moore, ed. New York, Van Nostrand, 1867, 12 Vols.

Revised Laws and Ordinances of the City of Troy. Troy, Tuttle, Belcher & Burton, 1876.

RICKER, MARY SWING, "Uncle Sam in Cartoon." *Hearst's International Magazine*, Vol. 19 (1910), p. 1091.

ROURKE, CONSTANCE, *American Humor, A Study of the National Character*. New York, Harcourt, 1931.

SCHACHNER, NATHAN, *The Founding Fathers*. New York, Putnam, 1954.

SCHEER, GEORGE F., and RANKIN, HUGH F., *Rebels and Redcoats*. Cleveland, World, 1957.

SHAW, ALBERT, *A Cartoon History of Roosevelt's Career*. New York, Review of Reviews Co., 1910.

———— *Abraham Lincoln, His Path to the Presidency*. New York, Review of Reviews Co., 1929.

SMITH, SAMUEL ABBOTT, *West Cambridge on the Nineteenth of April, 1775*. Boston, Alfred Mudge, 1864, reprinted 1955.

SONNECK, OSCAR G. T., *Report on "the Star Spangled Banner," "Hail Columbia," "America," "Yankee Doodle."* Washington, U. S. Government Printing Office, 1909.

SWANSON, NEIL H., *The Perilous Fight*. New York, Farrar & Rinehart, 1945.

TYLER, ROYALL, *The Contrast: a comedy in five acts*. Boston, Houghton, 1920.

VERNON, GRENVILLE, *Yankee Doodle-doo, a collection of songs of the early American Stage*. New York, Payson & Clarke Ltd., 1927.

WALSH, WILLIAM S., *Abraham Lincoln and the London* Punch. New York, Moffat, Yard, 1909.

WEISE, ARTHUR JAMES, *City of Troy and Its Vicinity*. Troy, Edward Green, 1886.

———— *History of the City of Troy*. Troy, William H. Young, 1876.

———— *Troy's One Hundred Years*. Troy, William H. Young, 1891.

WEITENKAMPF, FRANK, "Our Political Symbols." *New York History,* Cooperstown, Vol. 33, No. 4 (October 1952), pp. 371-378.

———— *Political Caricature in the United States, 1787–1898*. New York, New York Public Library, 1953.

———— *Uncle Sam Through the Years, A Cartoon Record*. New York, Typescripts at New York Historical Society, and New York Public Library, 1949.

WERTENBAKER, THOMAS J., *Father Knickerbocker Rebels, New York City During the Revolution*. New York, Scribner, 1948.

WILMER, LAMBERT A., *Our Press Gang*. Philadelphia, J. T. Lloyd, 1860.

WILSON, RUFUS ROCKWELL, *Lincoln in Caricature*. New York, Horizon, 1929.

"Wilson, Samuel," in *Dictionary of American Biography* (New York), Vol. 20.

"Wilson, Samuel," in *New York State Historical Association Quarterly Journal* (January 1929), pp. 97-98.

WOODWORTH, JOHN, *Reminiscences of Troy from Its Settlement in 1790 to 1807*. Albany, J. Munsell, 1860.

Works of Thomas Jefferson, The, Paul Leicester Ford, ed. New York, Putnam, 1892-99, 10 Vols.

PERIODICALS

American Weekly Messenger, Vol. II (Philadelphia, March 26–Sept. 17, 1814).

Brother Jonathan (New York, January–August, 1842).

The Examiner, Vol. II (New York, May–October, 1814).

Harper's Weekly (New York, 1859-65, also scattered issues to 1900).

Leslie's Weekly (various issues, mainly of the Civil War period).

Life, Vol. XLVIII (July–December, 1906), also Vol. LI (January–June, 1908).

Literary Digest, Vol. LVII (April–June, 1918), also Vol. LIX (October–December, 1918).

Puck (scattered issues, mainly of the 1880's and 1890's).

Punch (London, 1841-97).

Punchinello (for the Civil War period).

Uncle Sam's Almanac (scattered issues, from the 1840's and 1850's).

Vanity Fair (for the Civil War period).

NEWSPAPERS

For Troy, N.Y., sources: *Troy Northern Budget, Troy Times,* and *Troy Record.*

For War of 1812 period generally: New York *Impartial Gazeteer,* New York *Independent Journal and General Advertiser,* New York *National Advocate,* New York *American Minerva,* Boston *Columbian Centinel, Albany Gazette,* and *Albany Republican.*

For Elbert Anderson's death notice and the story by the "eye-witness" to Uncle Sam's christening in his new role: New York *Advertiser,* New York *Gazette,* New York *Journal of Commerce,* New York *American,* New York *Morning Courier,* New York *Evening Post,* New York *Statesman and Advertiser,* and *Troy Budget* (April and May, 1830 issues).

For Civil War period: New York *Times,* New York *Herald,* New York *Tribune;* also Confederate papers, Richmond *Dispatch,* Richmond *Enquirer,* and Charleston *Mercury.*

Index

Actualités, 76
Adams, John, 17, 42
Aesop, 20
Agitprop, 113
Akin, James, 65
Albany, N. Y., 50
Albany *Evening Journal,* 58
Albany Knickerbocker News, xi
Albany Times Union, x
Allen, Harriet Maria, 43
Alphonse and Gaston, 98
Anderson, Elbert, Jr., 38, 39, 40, 43
Annuit coeptis, 21
Arlington, Mass., viii, 45, 130
Ashley's Tavern, 36
Atlas Universel, 11

Baldwin, Stanley, 121
Baltimore American, 127
Baltimore *Sun,* 117
Bank of the United States, 61, 63, 64, 67, 92
Bartlett, John Russell, 25, 27
Barton, William, 20
Batchelor, G. C., 110
Batherick, Mother, 46
Beauregard, G. P. T., Gen., 84
Beaverbrook, Lord, 108, 121

Belisarius, 6
Belknap, Rufus, 56
Bellew, Frank H. T., 61, 66, 95
Ben Day, 85
Benton, Thomas, 62
Berryman, Jim, 109
Berteaux, 17
Biddle, Nicholas, 62, 64
Blaine, James G., 97
Bonaparte, Napoleon, 41, 68
Boston *Gazette,* 15
Boudinot, Elias, 20
Bricker, John, 109
Brinton, Crane, 117
Britannia, 6, 15, 24, 71
Brookline, N. H., 130
Brother Jonathan, 27-34, 60, 62, 63, 65, 66, 67, 70, 71, 72-77, 80, 95
Brother Jonathan (weekly), 32
Brown, John, 45
Buchanan, George, 60
Bucholzer, H., 66
Bull Moose Party, 93
Bush, C. G., 96

Candido, 115
Calhoun, John C., 66, 67

California, offer to buy, 68, elephant emblem of, 92
Cardenio, 5
Cass, Lewis, 67
Cassell, John, 102
Catskill, N. Y., 54-56
Chamberlain, Neville, 9
Chapman, John, 49
Charles, William, 31
Charleston, W. Va., *Gazette,* 1
Chase, Salmon P., 22, 126
Churchill, Winston, 4
Clay, Edward W., 63, 66, 68, 69
Clay, Henry, 44, 64, 66, 92
Cleveland, Grover, 100
Cohan, George M., 120
Columbia, 23, 24, 78, 88, 89, 92
Columbian Centinel, 35
Columbus, O., *Dispatch,* 104
Communism, 88, propaganda, 112-117
Concord, Mass., battle of, 46, 47
Concord, N. H., 56
Contrast, The, 29
Cooper's Tavern, 47
Country Lovers, The, 29
Crawford, Thomas, 33
Creel, George, 103
Crockett, Davy, 93
Crosby, Percy L., 107
Currier and Ives, 77
Curtis, George William, 89
Cutter Family, 45

Daladier, Edouard, 9
Dalrymple, Louis, 100
Darling, J. N., 107
Davenport, Homer, 99, 100
Davis, Jefferson, 33, 84-86
Dearborn, Henry, Gen., 37, 42
De Bry, Théodore, 10
Decatur, Comm. Stephen, 31
Deccan Herald, 117
Declaration of Independence, 17
De Pompadour, Mme., 11
De Vaugondy, Robert, 11
Dewey, Thomas, 109
Dickens, Charles, 111
Donkey, Democratic, 64
Don Quixote, 26
Doolittle, Amos, 31, 47
Douglas, Stephen A., 78
Downing, Major Jack, 62, 90
Doyle, Dickie, 71

Duffy, Edmund, 107
Dunne, Finley Peter, 63
Du Simitière, Eugène Pierre, 18

Eagle as U. S. emblem, 20, 21, 22, 126
Elephant, Republican, 90
Embargo, The, 29
Enright, Walter J., 15
Epictetus, 7
E pluribus unum, 19
Eustis, William, 38
Eye of Providence, 19, 21, 126

Fairburn, John, 23
Father Time, 15
Fitzpatrick, Daniel, 105
Flagg, James Montgomery, 102
Fowle, Samuel A., 45
Fowle's Mill, 45, 46
France, indemnity from, 68
Frank Leslie's Illustrated Newspaper, 77
Franklin, Benjamin, 6, 14, 16, 17, 22, 78, 93, 126
Franz Ferdinand, Archduke of Austria, 101
Freedom, Statue of, 33

Gadsden Purchase, 68
Gage, Gen. Thomas, 48
Gandhi, 5
Garfield, James A., 96
Gentleman's Journal, The, 19
Gentleman's Magazine, The, 19
Gibson, Charles Dana, 104
Gillray, James, 6, 121
Gleason, Jonas W., 54, 55
Glidden, George K., 44
Goff, Frederick R., 42
Golden, James J., 130
Gottfried, Johann Ludwig, 10
Grant, Ulysses S., 32, 87
Greenbush military camp, 35

Hail Columbia, 25
Hancock, Gen. Winfield S.; 96
Happy Hooligan, 98
Harding, Warren G., 105
Harlequin, 26
Harper, Fletcher, 87, 89
Harper, J. W. Jr., 89
Harper's Weekly, 2, 86, 87, 90, 95, 98, 133
Harrison, William Henry, 37, 64, 93
Hart Tavern, 36
Hartford Convention, 33